In the Spirit of Marriage

In the Spirit of Marriage

Creating and Sustaining Loving Unions

Robert Roskind

CELESTIALARTS
Berkeley / Toronto

CELESTIALARTS

P.O. Box 7123
Berkeley, California 94707
www.tenspeed.com

Distributed in Canada by Ten Speed Press Canada, in the United Kingdom and Europe by Airlift Books, in New Zealand by Southern Publishers Group, in Australia by Simon & Schuster Australia, in South Africa by Real Books, and in Singapore, Malaysia, Hong Kong, and Thailand by Berkeley Books.

Cover design by Betsy Stromberg
Interior design by Jeff Puda and Larissa Pickens

Library of Congress Control Number: 00-136237

ISBN 0-89087-991-5

First Celestial Arts printing, 2001
Printed in Canada

1 2 3 4 5 6 7—05 04 03 02 01

Dedication

To Julia—my wife, my friend, my teacher, my coworker

Contents

Introduction

*F*or most of my life, my romantic intimate relationships were a mixture of pleasure and pain, clarity and confusion, harmony and tension. When I met my wife, Julia, twenty years ago, this pattern continued into our marriage. I think this is the way it is with most people and I think this is the way it has always been, going all the way back to Adam and Eve. Marriages (by "marriages" I mean all mated relationships) have usually been a mixed bag, especially after the honeymoon period has lost its glow.

At some point in the first few years of our marriage, Julia and I thought there might be a better way. We started with the premise that many marriages, ours included, might not be as satisfying and peaceful as they could be because we were misunderstanding their true purpose, their real function. We thought that perhaps if we redefined our marriage's purpose and we viewed it from a new perspective, it would work better. We have and it did.

We began to understand that our relationship's true function was to teach us how to love each other unconditionally. It was, and is, simply a teaching aid to teach love. We still hit our hard places. However, the key difference now is that conflicts occur with much less frequency and last for a much shorter duration before peace is again restored to our relationship. A change in our perspective has created a change in our relationship.

Being a teacher, I wanted to share this new perspective. This book is about what we learned.

This is not another self-help book. It is not my intention to tell you how to fix or correct or adjust your existing relationship so that it will work better. Rather, the intention of this book is to offer you a new perspective, a new paradigm, by which to view your relationship, your mate, and yourself. This book is a guide to help you see all three through the eyes of unconditional love. Once you have incorporated this perspective into your thoughts and feelings, your relationships will make the needed adjustments. Having changed the cause (your thoughts and feelings), the effects (your relationships) will change automatically and immediately.

This book is for everyone, whether they are mated, single, separated, or divorced. However, for each group, the book's impact may be different. If you are presently mated, this book will help you make your existing relationship more intimate, peaceful, and loving. If you are single and seeking a life mate, this book will help you in uncovering, and resolving, any fears or barriers that may be preventing you from creating and sustaining a loving mated relationship. If you are considering a divorce or separation, this book will offer no pat answers but will encourage you to follow your own guidance. It may even help in transforming the separation into union again. On the other hand, should you decide to separate, this book will help you do so with greater love and clarity.

Your progress towards a happier relationship may be much faster than Julia's and mine. My hope is that much of the peace concerning intimate relationships that I have found after a twenty-year struggle can be effectively transferred to you in the few hours it takes to read this book.

A Personal Odyssey

On April 9, 1980, on my thirty-third birthday, I met my wife, Julia. For both of us, our meeting was a watershed event in our emotional, mental, and spiritual growth. Our previous romantic relationships, though at the time loving and clear, had been heavily influenced by our fears. For the most part, they were fear-based. Our relationship was the first one for either of us that was predominantly love-based. It was not that we had finally gotten lucky enough or wise enough to find the right partner. Rather, it was that we were both finally deciding to choose love over fear. I would like to tell you about a realization I had a month before I met my wife. This realization was the final piece in the puzzle for understanding why I had not been getting what I wanted in my love life.

I was living in the San Francisco Bay Area and running a nonprofit organization that offered house-building and remodeling classes to home owners throughout northern California. After a fulfilling day at my office (and almost all my workdays were fulfilling), I returned to my apartment in Berkeley. At that time, I was "between relationships" and the emptiness of my apartment engulfed me as I ate my dinner and contemplated yet another evening alone. Though I had come to terms with being on my own to the point that it no longer drove me into messy relationships or frantic social adventures, I still greatly desired to share my life with someone.

As I sat there over my greasy take-out chicken dinner, I could not help but notice the vast difference between my days at work and my nights at home. At work I seemed to always get what I wanted and needed, sometimes even "miraculously" creating just the right solution to a problem. My work was much of what I had hoped it would be, i.e., fulfilling, successful, filled with friends, and of benefit to others. In stark contrast, my home life was nothing of what I had hoped it would be. It was lonely, unfulfilling, and without the human warmth and communication that makes a house a home. I think we are all like this, creating "success" in one area of our life and not in others. Some are excellent parents, but their finances are in disarray. Some have success in their careers, but failures in their relationships, etc.

That night I resolved to understand what accounted for this vast discrepancy in these two areas of my life. This was no longer the rhetorical question that it had been for so many years. I really wanted to know why I had been able to create success in one area of my life and not in another.

Though I had asked the question countless times, this time I thought I might be able to find the answer. Usually when I asked, "Why have I still not found a loving relationship?" I was only wallowing in self-pity. However, now I did really want to know the answer, and because I did, the answer was immediately clear.

As I sat at the kitchen table, it hit me. The answer was so obvious, I could not believe I had not seen it before. I cannot remember now what the answer was, but at the time it was crystal clear. Hopefully, one day I will remember and can share it with my readers. (Just kidding.) Here is what I realized. The essential difference between these two areas of my life was that my work life was predominantly influenced by my confidence and my trust, and my love life predominantly by my fears. Two very different belief systems (all my thoughts, feelings, beliefs, fears, etc.) were creating two very different realities.

I had been developing each of these different beliefs since my youth. My belief system concerning work, dominated by mostly positive thoughts and feelings, reflected back my faith that I could be successful in this area of my life. Therefore, my external success at work was reflecting back to me my internal beliefs that I could be successful in this area of my life. My early ventures into the world of business had been successful and encouraging. Also, since I came from a long line of successful business people, and did well in school and business, the outside world gave me the feedback that helped to solidify my belief that I could succeed in this area.

My love life was also reflecting back to me my belief system. However, unlike my work life, my dominant thoughts in this area of my life were ones of fear regarding finding a life mate. Though I had always hoped to meet her, I also feared I would never do so. The faith and fear battled inside me, with the fear usually dominating. Rather than a belief system built largely on faith, it was primarily fear-based. My early forays into young love were bittersweet. I experienced both acceptance and rejection. Since I possessed neither striking good looks, nor great athletic prowess, nor romantic self-confidence, the key assets for males in early romantic relationships, the outside world did not always offer me definite support that I would succeed in this area.

In both my work life and love life, I was simply creating my external reality from my internal belief system. One reflected my faith, the other my fear. In both cases my "prayers" (my thoughts and feelings) were being answered. My relationships were reflecting the mixture of both my fears and my faith, with the dominant of the two setting the overall tone. In my work life my dominant belief system was faith in success. In my love life it was fear of failure.

Realizing this that night was like a great "Aha!!" The pain of one too many lonely nights had finally caused me to seek and reveal to myself my long-standing and self-defeating inner programming. Immediately, I understood that I only needed to have faith that I would meet someone, and that I was worthy of a loving relationship and home. I realized I only had to change my thoughts and feelings to change my world.

As I sat there, another thought became clear. By now I was beginning to accept the reality of a loving God and I realized that such a Creator would not have endowed us with such a strong yearning for a loving mate without also giving us the ability to create one. Only a cruel God would cause such frustration, if the means did not accompany the desire. Surely we were not meant to live a life of frustration and loneliness, never being able to satisfy an almost universal human desire. I realized that my fears were keeping God's gift of love from me.

I decided that night to redirect my thoughts and feelings as much as I possibly could. I began to trust that I deserved a loving relationship, that this was everyone's birthright. We all have been created to love and be loved, in any form we truly desire. I realized that I did not need to be perfect to be loved. I decided that though I had no idea how much longer it might be until I met her (weeks, months, or years), I would just relax and enjoy myself, knowing she was heading toward me as I was heading toward her.

In the weeks that followed, the apartment seemed much less lonely. Going out with mated friends did not heighten my loneliness as it had done before. Saturday nights alone were bearable, almost enjoyable. And though I cannot say all fears were gone, they had been greatly reduced and were no longer dominant. When they did resurface, my newly found revelations allowed me to release them. I started to have imaginary conversations with this person that I knew was heading toward me. I even began to visualize her eyes. A month later I met my wife.

No luck was involved in our meeting. Nor were we being rewarded by a judgmental God. We had both, independently, reduced our fears regarding a mated relationship to the point where they no longer dominated. They fears still existed, but our dominant thoughts and feelings were that we deserved and could have a loving relationship. Our belief systems, reflecting greater love and trust than fear, had begun to create a new reality and, therefore, a new relationship for both of us.

Both of us still brought certain fears, certain unhealed wounds, to this new relationship. We are still very much involved in transforming our relationship into a "healed relationship." Even as this book goes to print, there are times when one or both of us blames the other for our momentary unhappiness or in other ways projects our anger or fears onto the other. However, fear is no longer dominant for either of us. As more and more healing and release from fear occurs, the more peaceful our relationship becomes. In many ways, our relationship has become a spiritual path unto itself.

Chapter 1

The Stages of Marriage

*R*ecently a large Midwestern university did an intensive study on the stages of marriage and each stage's average length. They defined these stages as follows:

1) Illusion (average length: two months)
2) Disillusion (average length: two years)
3) Misery (average length: thirty years)
4) Mutual respect (remainder of marriage)
5) Bliss (remainder of marriage)

So now the data is officially in. This research also explains why divorce rates tend to peak around the second and third year of marriage, when disillusionment sinks in. The average couple gets two months of illusional happiness followed by two years of disillusionment and then thirty years of misery before they get any more bliss. And the research further showed that many marriages never make it to Stages 4 and 5! I do not know about you, but this just does not seem like a particularly good deal to me. Maybe three or five years of pain, maybe I could even see ten years. But thirty-two years! No wonder so many people just go around grabbing the few months of illusion in Stage 1 and then go on to the next relationship. I mean, can you really blame them? For crying out loud, is this system not working or what!

For the purposes of this book, I have "condensed" the five stages discussed in the research to three stages. The first stage is the exciting and thrilling honeymoon period. This is the same as the "illusion stage" of the research. This usually lasts from several weeks to several years (I have had a few that only lasted a few nights). During this phase, we are sure all our wounds will be magically and effortlessly healed by this relationship, and this bliss will endure for a lifetime. We are convinced our mate is near perfect. Our long night of loneliness is finally over, and that "special someone" has finally seen our true beauty and we have seen theirs. We have finally found the source of our true happiness and peace.

I will refer to this initial romantic stage as the "special love relationship." It is special because we believe our happiness resides just with that particular person. We are now offering "special" love to our mate and our mate only. It is for them and no one else. They are special and deserve it. We feel they see our "specialness" and will offer us their "special" love in return. In addition, this relationship is even more "special" because it, unlike all others, offers us true happiness. It is "special" in its ability to really make us happy. Special, special, special, the ego's mantra.

During this illusional Stage 1, we believe that our mate and our relationship are the source of our happiness. In this intoxicated and delusional stage we make all kinds of promises and decisions, including that we want to spend the rest of our lives with this person. Can you think of any state less likely to lead to a good decision than the stage of being passionately, head over heels in love? About half of our love songs are written about this stage (just another codependent love song, sung in three-part harmony). However, if this is the stage you are in, put this book down immediately! You really do not want to know what may be ahead in the later stages. Go out and indulge yourself in your passion and joy and then read the rest, if your relationship changes.

Now, for the rest of us, let us continue. After the honeymoon period ends, usually to our dismay and disappointment, the relationship begins to enter the "disillusionment stage" and finally enters the painful "misery stage." These two combined are my "Stage 2" or "special hate relationship." Do not let the word "hate" offend you. Actually, hate is only fear, anger, and pain expressing itself as "hate." This stage is defined by our judgments of others, which include an element of hate. The definition of hate is "to feel great aversion for." At times during Stage 2 this is what we feel toward our mate.

Unlike the blissful Stage 1, Stage 2 involves power struggles, conflict, judgment, stress, disappointment, frustration, and blame. This stage is not much fun. It usually begins with a few isolated events. They did not call when they said, they seemed unconcerned during talk at dinner, their political views are all wrong, they are too neat or too sloppy, they got mad over something insignificant, our best friend did not think they were so great, they did not want to make love, they were too critical, they seemed interested in another person, they belched. It can be anything. It begins like a small leak in a dam. At first, we think, "Nothing to worry about, we will correct all that stuff in time." But after awhile we begin to fear we are seeing a pattern emerge. There is another leak, and another, and another. Pretty soon there are more leaks than we have fingers, and after awhile the entire dam bursts. Stage 2 has fully reared its ugly head. We begin to wonder if we have married a total jerk.

At times these painful feelings seem to be gone, and Stage 1 pleasantly returns. Whew, it was only a false alarm. They really are something special. I really am happy here. Nothing to worry about. But actually the feelings are not gone, only submerged. Denying them only becomes more and more difficult. Another situation occurs, another button gets pushed, and up the judgments pop, becoming more familiar with each new appearance.

It is during this painful period that we fear there is something inherently wrong with us, or our mate, or our relationship, or perhaps all three. During Stage 2, we begin to seriously doubt that our mate can, or is willing to, truly love us. We begin to wonder if perhaps we made a bad choice. Perhaps they were not as perfect and emotionally well-adjusted as we initially believed. Or, on the other hand, we may begin to blame our-selves. Perhaps we are incapable of creating and maintaining the loving relationship we had envisioned.

Stage 2 begins to appear when we realize that Stage 1 is not going to bring us the happiness we thought. Once Stage 2 is fully ushered in, we may come to believe our mate and our relationship are the source of our unhappiness. This perception only serves to keep us trapped in our pain and loneliness. The other half of the love songs are written about this stage. Few marriages ever leave this second stage. If they do, it is usually after wallowing in it for decades.

For awhile the relationship will swing between special love and special hate. Between the fights and hard places there are peaceful, perhaps wonderful times. Some days it is hard to remember why we thought they were so screwed up only the day before. Other days we have a hard time remembering what we ever saw in them. As this happens, the relation-ship is not always experienced as painful or the pain may only be experi-enced as mild irritation or boredom. However, during this swing between the two stages, the special love relationship will create illusions, and their corresponding codependency. The special hate relationship will leave wounds unhealed and festering.

The healed relationship is the third stage (the same as Stages 4 and 5 combined in the research). In this stage we can become free of the pen-dulum ride between special love and special hate (which all too often gets stuck in special hate). It is in this stage that the relationship reaches its full potential and offers both people the joining and peace they seek. It is in this stage that we learn to love another unconditionally. This book is a guide through Stages 1 and 2 and into Stage 3.

Most relationships must go through the first two stages in order to enter this final fulfilling Stage 3. This is normal. The romantic Stage 1 can be enjoyed and cherished as it provides the foundation of bonding needed for the later stages. Also, there is nothing "wrong" with you, your mate, or your relationship because you have been stuck in the pain of Stage 2. This painful stage is part of our healing process. Most people go through Stages 1 and 2. There are, however, those who never go through Stage 1, as well as a few rare relationships that begin and remain in Stage 3.

These stages are not always experienced distinctly and in a linear order. We may be experiencing any two, or all three, stages at any given period in our relationship. It is very common for Stages 1 and 2 to overlap, as it is for Stages 2 and 3. We may well feel the romantic intensity of Stage 1 towards our mate one day, the judgment of Stage 2 the next, and the unconditional love of Stage 3 later the same day.

We do not need to avoid special love relationships. In fact, we cannot. Every relationship we form will be done so by our egos, and will therefore be special. However, these relationships can become healed, if we are willing to continually ask that it be transformed and used to teach unconditional love. Indeed, the true function of a special love or hate relationship is as a "teaching aid" to teach the unconditional love of a healed relationship. The special relationship reveals to us our fears, our illusions, and our idols. These relationships then give us the opportunity to correct these perceptions, to change our belief system, and in so doing we begin to learn and teach love. When we do this, we reveal once again the healed relationship that has always existed within the illusion of the special relationship.

The Miracle of Stage 3

Now I know I have been mentioning unconditional love a lot here. You are probably sick of the term by now and it is only the beginning of the book. But bear with me. I think you have a pretty good idea what it means. But since the whole premise of the book rests on the attainment of this lofty goal, maybe I had better define exactly what I mean by the term.

Unconditional love is just what it says—love with no conditions. That means love is extended with no desire for the other person to change, or to act, or to be different than they already are. It means accepting them completely as they are. Our love is not diminished or conditioned by our desire to have them be different or better. Nor is our love conditional on what they, or the relationship, give to us. We do not love them because they make us feel loved, or needed, or wanted, or secure, or less lonely, or happy, or attractive, etc. Unconditional love seeks only to express itself without regard for what is given back.

By now you may be thinking, "You want me to love my mate (mother, father, boss, coworker, etc.) unconditionally?! No way. Even God has trouble loving them unconditionally!" Does this sound difficult, perhaps impossible? You betcha. But what could be more difficult than the present state of human life on this planet, which usually reflects conditional love, if any love at all? And what could be more impossible than allowing this to continue ad nauseam, as we have in the past? I do not know about you, but I have just about had it and from where I sit, unconditional love seems to be about the only thing that will make any real change.

Unconditional love can create change because as we learn to love our mates, in spite of their "flaws," their attacks, their unloving behavior, their insecurities, their betrayals, their inconsideration, etc., we have restored to our relationship its true, perhaps its holy, function: to learn to love another, and ourselves, unconditionally. When we do this in any relationship, we begin to share a common goal; we begin to perceive another's interests as equal to our own. Our mate longs to be loved unconditionally, and we desire to love them this way. We long to be loved unconditionally, and they long to love us that way. Our goals have become equal and the same. We both want to love and be loved, unconditionally. We have begun to practice the Golden Rule: to love another as ourselves. Until then, our goals are separate and divided. Each person is in the relationship for what they want. This is the source of the pain of Stage 2.

The Conscious Marriage

Stages 1 and 2 are "unconscious" relationships. By this I mean that many of the forces that effect these relationships are operating at an unconscious level within us. In these stages we are not yet consciously aware of what these forces are. In Stage 1, we do not consciously choose whom we fall in love with or who falls in love with us. It just "happens." In Stage 2, though we often think we understand why we are in a painful power struggle, usually our conflicts are created by past unhealed wounds and conditioning that are not consciously apparent to us. It is during Stage 3 that we often begin to understand the inner dynamics that are creating these issues. As we begin to enter Stage 3, these dynamics begin to be not only fully understood, but also resolved.

Now, in the healed marriage, we deliberately choose to align our interests with those of our mate. We begin to consciously choose to act and respond lovingly. This becomes a conscious act of our will, not an automatic, unconscious response. Love is as love does. Our new goal is now set and its achievement assured. The relationship becomes a context to perceive the other's inner spiritual perfection (forget about human perfection, it is a contradiction in terms) and to remind them of this Divine quality. We choose to see "the light, not the lampshade."

It is this inner quality, our reality of our innocence as a Child of God, that is always worthy of unconditional love. Our unconditional love offers the other the healing that they have been seeking. And by offering it, we heal ourselves. This "healed" relationship then becomes the pattern for the way in which we strive to love everyone. No matter what the form of our relationship is, the content, which is unconditional love, remains the same. Though we may love one person as a mate, another as a child, another as a friend, and still another as a stranger, we strive to love them all unconditionally. However, remember the accomplishment of a healed relationship is a lifelong process, not a specific event. It is a long-distance run, not a sprint. So pace yourself accordingly and above all be gentle with yourself.

Only at Stage 3, the healed relationship, do our emotions, and subsequent choices, come under our "conscious" control. Now the relationship begins to reflect our conscious emotional clarity and we are able to choose to respond with love. We are able and willing to see another through the eyes of love. We no longer feel we are the "effect" of our relationship.

We are the "cause" of it. We have loosened the grip of our unconscious fears. We have regained our freedom to consciously choose. We have taken the control away from our fears and returned it to its rightful owner, our Love.

However, before we get too carried away here, let us get back to the present. OK, now. Most of us are still struggling in Stage 2, and although we may have even given up on the hope of ever attaining the third stage, it is possible to reach it. It only requires three conditions. In fact, our willingness to continually recommit to these conditions assures that we will reach it.

Three Conditions Necessary to Create a Healed Relationship

1) Both partners must be committed to the relationship and their partner's growth.
2) Both partners must be committed to the process of seeking a deeper stage of joining and love. They must believe there is "a better way."
3) Both partners must be willing to accept the common goal of seeing the other's interests as equal to their own (the Golden Rule: "Love your neighbor as yourself").

You may want to read once again these three conditions and be sure you are clear on what they are. Please note the words "seeking" in #2 and "willing" in #3. We were looking for intention here, not perfection. Now, some of you might be thinking, "I am willing to do all this, but I am not so sure that that unenlightened mate of mine is." I am not going to lie to you. This is a dilemma. Should only one person in the relationship makes these commitments, at a deep level the relationship has become spiritually "healed," though not emotionally and mentally healed. Only one of the participants is choosing to accept the greater peace of the new relationship. The gift of peace of the healed relationship still awaits the other's willingness to receive it. Often a one-sided commitment may well create the environment that will bring the other person along. This is often the course the journey to a healed relationship takes, with one person initially committing to a new goal and the other subsequently choosing it.

However, each person must decide for themselves how long they are willing to remain in a marriage waiting for another to "wake up" and choose and accept the gift of peace. The other may still need to remain asleep in a fearful relationship, not wanting to yet awaken. A love-based relationship may still present too great a threat to their fear-based belief system.

However, setting a goal of a healed relationship, even by just one person, can greatly diminish the possibility of divorce or separation. If the union is salvageable, unconditional love will do the trick.

Accomplishing a healed relationship is not an easy task. It takes a tremendous amount of honest self-examination and willingness to have our wounds exposed and healed. After we have projected our blame onto our mates, we must be willing to take it back and see it is our stuff, not theirs. This can be frightening and painful to do and many people would rather leave a relationship than do it. Both partners must be committed to each other and this tremendous work, if it is to succeed. Again, it is a process, not an event. If any of the three conditions are missing, by either partner, the relationship's progress toward the fulfillment of a healed state will be impeded until the commitments are embraced again. Often this process is unnecessarily delayed for the life of the marriage. It never need be.

Chapter 2

The Healed Marriage:
Returning to the Garden

*D*id you ever wonder, way back in Sunday school when you first heard the story of the Garden of Eden, why Adam and Eve and all humans since were banished from the Garden just because they "ate from the Tree of Knowledge of good and evil, right and wrong"? For such a small infraction, we were booted out of a safe and peaceful reality into a hostile and pain-filled world. I mean, it was not like they killed anybody or anything. They just ate a piece of fruit. The punishment just does not seem to fit the crime. Did God not seem to be overreacting a little bit? After all, if my nine-year-old daughter disobeys me and plays with her guinea pig on the bed, I do not lock her in the basement for the rest of her life. Come on, admit it, did that not just seem like a strange thing for God to do?

However, maybe rather than a punishment from God, this event just represented the principle that we have been discussing, that whatever we believe we create. Let me explain. Maybe as soon as we started to judge and condemn others (and ourselves), or, metaphorically, as soon as we ate the fruit of this tree of good and evil, we lost our peace, our Garden of Eden. We began to compare, judge, and condemn. We decided that some people were better than others; that some people needed to be corrected and "fixed"; that some things, situations, and people were good or bad, right or wrong. Perhaps we were not thrown out of the Garden, but chose to leave on our own by our judging and condemning.

The healed relationship described in this chapter is the "return to the Garden." Within this Garden lies our peace and our happiness. It is in a healed marriage that we begin to stop judging our mates and trying to "fix" them and begin to unconditionally love them as they are. However, we must also realize that when we ask to see our mates through the eyes of unconditional love, we are also asking that all our wounds, our fears, our insecurities, etc., be revealed to us. These are the barriers to us loving unconditionally. This can be an intense and sometimes painful process. We must further understand that creating a healed relationship is not an event, but rather a lifelong process. Perhaps another metaphor would be helpful here.

Imagine that for years you have looked at a beautiful garden full of flowers, trees, meadows, babbling brooks, beautiful waterfalls, all bright and serene. Its peace and beauty calls to you and you long to enter. At some deep level you sense it is the Home you have always sought. However, blocking your entrance is a large, locked metal gate (fear). You have tried many keys in the gate (pleasuring, owning, power, accomplishing, impressing, belonging, relationships, etc.). Though occasionally the door seemed to open for a moment, allowing you entrance to this peaceful and loving world, it has always slammed shut again, sometimes catching your fingers and causing pain.

Finally, you find a box that says "This will open the gate" (true forgiveness and the healed relationship). In joy and anticipation you open the box expecting to find a key. In just moments you will be inside the garden you have longed to enter. Soon you will be Home! Believing you have found a key, you think all you have to do is insert it in the lock and open the gate. It will be quick and easy. As you open the box, to your dismay, there is not a key, only a small file.

You soon realize that rather than entering the garden in one triumphant burst, it will take a long series of small actions, repeated every day until we have finally loosened the bars. These actions are our everyday attempts to teach and learn love and forgiveness. They are our ongoing process to release our judgment and condemnations as they arise and to ask that they be transformed through the eyes of love. Each stroke of the file may appear mundane and unimportant, yet each one is necessary and none can be avoided.

Do not become disheartened. Each stroke of the file, each attempt to forgive and love, loosens the bars and the grip the world's thinking has on our minds. Many times it may appear that we have made one step forward and two backwards, but trust that the direction is always toward freedom.

And the funny thing is, we find that once we are finally inside, we will turn around and see that though there was a gate, there was no wall. We were never really blocked from the garden. It was only an illusion. Then we notice that the garden extends everywhere we see, on both sides of the gate. We were never not in the garden. That was also just an illusion.

Marriage: Past, Present, and Future

Let's face it, for most of us marriage has not turned out exactly as we had expected. This is probably the greatest unspoken disappointment of our generation. We have been willing to admit to, and discuss, many of our other disillusionments, with war, with government, with medicine, with education, with the environment, with the food and water sources, with institutions and churches, with our parents, with the workplace, with our bodies, etc. In most of these areas we have rationally looked at the reasons these systems are not working and are developing new paradigms that offer great hope for the future. But there is little public conversation on how tremendously disappointed we are that our marriages have not worked out, usually causing more pain and disappointment than fulfillment and joy. There is little development of new paradigms in this area. I hope this book offers one.

Actually, on one level, marriages have never "worked." They may have worked socially, financially, religiously, and logistically, but they have seldom brought people the peace, joy, and love they had hoped for. This was as true in the past as it is in the present. Couples did not live "happily ever after," as we were told. Though in the past the divorce rate was lower, this was primarily due to religious, social, and economic factors, rather than the fact that the marriages were inherently more satisfying. We need to free ourselves from the mistaken belief that marriages in previous times were "better" just because they lasted longer. In the past, many people had much lower expectations of the marriages. Past generations have been more willing to remain in their marriages and let go of their fantasies (if they had any) and accept the marriage's reality.

Many of us were led to believe that we would meet Mr. or Ms. Right and begin our life of marital bliss together. For most of us, it has not worked out this way. Many of us have made marital happiness one of our most important goals, if not the most important goal. This concept is rather new in human evolution. In the past, marriages involved mostly convenience, money, customs, and childbearing and daily survival functions. In many cultures with arranged marriages, people do not actually meet their mates until the wedding day. Marriage has not been about happiness, but survival.

However, it must be understood that ours is the first generation in history to be freed from having survival and security as our primary focus. Our parents' generation was a "transitional" generation. Most were born into conditions where survival was the main issue. They later became stable or affluent and created an infrastructure so that the first generation ever, our own, would be raised free from the ancient necessity of directing most of our life energy toward basic survival.

It is understandable that, once freed from this burden, we focused on seeking greater meaning in our lives. Love is often the first thing we focus on once we have filled our basic needs and begin to seek meaning. Seeking this true love through our romantic relationships is a necessary step on the path to finding it. It seems only logical that it would reside there. It also seems logical that the deepest level of joining with another would be through a sexual, romantic relationship. However, now it is time that we begin to examine some of these underlying premises, our beliefs if you will, about marriage and our search for true love.

We have only begun to have a public dialogue that examines the entire way we view marriage. My supposition is that in order for marriages to really "work," we must develop a whole new paradigm, an entirely new way of looking at marriage and our mates. Therefore, this is why this is really not a typical self-help book. I do not intend to tell you how to "fix" your marriage, but rather I hope to offer you an entirely different perception of it. So, let us take a look at the way we presently view our mates and our marriage and see perhaps if our underlying premises are the cause of some of the pain. To begin to find some "solutions," we must first determine what is at the root of the problem.

What Is the Purpose of a Marriage?

What is marriage for? It seems like a simple question, but in answering it correctly lie the seeds of much of the happiness and unhappiness we will experience on this earth. So, let's look at some of the reasons we marry. Let us start with the clearest reasons and work "down" from there. At our best, we marry to give and share love with another person and perhaps to create a loving family unit. The marriage is to provide us with the love we need and desire. There are other healthy reasons, such as companionship, inspiration, providing a balanced and stable home for children, sharing life's pleasures and setbacks, etc. Finally, there are reasons birthed from our fears and insecurities, rather than from our higher nature. These reasons include financial stability or gain, physical safety, "legitimizing" a pregnancy, impressing others, satisfying our sexual desires, making others happy, and escaping an unhappy situation elsewhere.

As we determine our reason for mating, we can begin to understand how these then determine how we perceive our mates. We tend to perceive our mates in many different ways. They may be viewed as our parent, our child, our lover, our friend, our coworker, our responsibility, our therapist, our patient, our provider, our rescuer, our taskmaster, our jailer, or any mixture of these. We may view them as a wonderful gift and blessing in our life or a punishment or mistake. In fact, we may hold several contradicting views in the course of a day.

We may see them as a test to be endured or a joy to be celebrated. They may be seen as a gift for our purity or as a punishment for our flaws. We may think we made a great choice and never, or almost never, regret it. We may think we made a bad choice because of our neurotic fears, our loneliness, or our bad judgment. We may view this choice as one we are not sure we would re-choose, and may in fact be re-choosing. Or we may feel we made a commitment that must be kept.

Now, let us examine these common purposes and functions. All of these views, whether based upon our fears or our clarity, define our mates in terms of what they give to us and which of our needs they fill. Therefore, we perceive marriage as "for getting" what we need and want. Perhaps it is this premise that marriages are "for getting" that is causing the pain. Perhaps changing the underlying premise would lessen the pain. Maybe marriages, rather than being "for getting," are "for giving." Let me explain.

Maybe all of the above perceptions mask our mate's true function in our life: that of a teacher, we (and they) have chosen for our most important, and often difficult, lesson. This lesson, though it may present itself in many forms, is always the same: to teach us to love others unconditionally. Stated differently, it is our mate's purpose to remind us of who we, and they, really are, beings of unconditional love hidden behind the veil of our fears.

But, you wonder, if we are beings of unconditional love, we sure do not seem to be acting like it. Well, there is a reason for that and the reason does not invalidate the premise. In order to love unconditionally, there is only one thing we must do: remove the blocks or barriers that prevent our unconditional love, our true nature, from expressing. These barriers are our unhealed wounds, our unresolved fears, our insecurities, our judgments, our anger, our hate, our annoyance, and our irritation, etc. It is all that stuff that makes us feel separate. Therefore, we do not need to "learn" to love unconditionally. Without these blocks, our love would just be there, no longer hidden behind the dark veil of our fears. We only need to get all the stuff out of the way. Our mates and our marriages can help us do this.

After we meet our mates, we will not live "happily ever after," nor should we. That entire premise was wrong. The only path to unconditional love is directly through our fears and pain. We cannot get out of the swamp without wading through the mud. Therefore, part of the true function of any marriage is to expose to us all our unhealed wounds, so we can heal them. Unhealed wounds are often not a pretty sight. They may have been festering for a long time. And when someone presses our wounds (our "buttons"), we hurt and get mad. In fact, we often choose as mates those best able to push our buttons just so they can be understood and disarmed. Because of this, during a healthy healing process there will be arguments and distancing from each other. The arguments, the stuck feelings, the judging and condemning, the feelings of separation and loneliness, all that painful stuff we hate in our relationship, are just teaching aids we can use in our healing process. And, like many physical healing processes, things often get more painful before they get better. When we ask to love another unconditionally, we are asking that all our wounds and blocks be exposed to us.

When we ask to love another unconditionally,
we are asking that all our wounds
and blocks be exposed to us.

So the reason marriages have so seldom brought deep happiness and peace is that we have assigned them the wrong function. It is as simple, and as complicated, as that. In addition to social, physical, and financial security, we have decided that the function of our marriage, and therefore of our spouse, is for them to give us the peace, joy, and love we have always wanted. We have decided its function is to meet our needs. Our marriages, therefore, are "for getting," not "for giving." Because of this, we are seeking love and peace outside ourselves where it cannot be found. Love and peace are attributes within us. They can only be found there.

No matter how we try to improve our marriage, no matter how we struggle to improve our communication, our sensitivity, our under- standing, our sexual life, etc., until we restore to our marriage its true function, it will not lead to the peace and love we are seeking.

If we try to use something for anything other than its true func- tion, it will only cause us frustration and pain, because it will not work effectively. If we try to use a car as a bulldozer, it will never work effec- tively. Bulldozing is not its function. If we try to use a knife as a saw, it will frustrate us. Sawing is not its function. Whereas our relation- ships are meant to be miraculous healing wands, able to restore har- mony where strife and pain previously existed, we have used them as hammers to alter and attack. We can change the wand, improve it and try harder and harder to make it serve the function of a hammer, but it will never work. When their true function is perceived, our relation- ships will serve their true purpose as "healing wands."

What Do We Really Want in a Marriage? The Choice Is Ours

At this point I have asked you to consider, and hopefully accept, one basic premise: that we are creating our marriages, and all our relation- ships, from our existing belief system. It follows then that in order to change our relationships, we need only to change our minds (our belief systems). I assume here that you do want to change your relationship or you would not be reading this book. However, realizing that we create our relationships is not enough. We need to decide exactly what we want from these relationships. Once we have decided, it then becomes clear what in our belief systems, in our minds, must change to create it. Now I know all this sounds rather oversimplified and in a complex world simple answers may seem naïve at best, invalid at worst. But I assure you this is neither.

All our relationships are being created by us on a moment-by-moment, day-by-day basis by our thoughts and feelings. We have yet to understand the true power and nature of our minds. Our minds are creating every instant and never "sleep." At some level, all our thoughts and beliefs are always producing form (relationships, sickness, miracles, situations, matter, etc.).

Because of this there are no "idle thoughts." All our thoughts, even our casual "idle" ones, are creating our internal and, therefore, our outer reality. It is estimated that we have over sixteen thousand thoughts every day, 90 percent of which are repetition. We can continue to allow our minds to wander and they will continue to miscreate. Or we can begin to assert control over them so that they will create the love and peace we desire. It is therefore essential that we regain control over these so that they may create the world and lives we consciously want, rather than the ones we are subconsciously, and unconsciously, making. Because we are given free will, we are free to choose and create either fear or love. It is only by continually choosing love, and releasing fears, that we gain control over our minds and their incredible power to create.

So, now we must ask ourselves that if we have created our present relationship (or lack of one), why have we created it? I mean, if we have created something that is not bringing us lots of joy and happiness, why did we create it? Now, determining this also sounds easy, but it is not. As we well know, trying to uncover what conscious and unconscious forces are at work within us is a very difficult and frustrating task. It demands honest self-examination and that is not exactly in big supply these days. What makes the task even more difficult is that what we think we want in our marriages may differ from what we emotionally, and often subconsciously, really want.

If we are not sure of what we really want in our marriages, we need only look at our existing marriage, or lack of one. This relationship is a window into our belief system regarding marriage. And the view through this window may be less than breathtaking. In fact, it might be downright dismal. Whatever we have presently created is what we have "chosen" to create. Do we want passion and excitement? Do we want to "lose ourselves" in another? Do we want pain and anguish? Do we want high drama and upset? Do we want attack and defense, counterattack and revenge? Do we want attachment and codependence? Do we want loneliness, separation, and isolation? If any of these fit a description of our relationship, then at some level, perhaps unconsciously and previously unnoticed, this is what we want and have chosen. But do not be horrified by the view. We can clean all that up. That is what this book is all about.

Unless we consciously decide on the goal of our marriage (or anything for that matter), we have no way to evaluate which actions support our goal and which sabotage it. We have no way to know when we have arrived at the goal, or even if we are heading in the right direction. Without this clear-cut goal, events and situations just happen, and the outcome can be anything—which may or may not bring us peace and happiness. The key question we must ask ourselves is, therefore, "What do I want to come from this relationship?" Making a clear decision and beginning to act on it is tremendously empowering.

Does It Take Two?

If we change and the other person does not seem to outwardly change, we will experience the relationship differently. It will have changed for us. At a deeper level, though not always observable, the other person will have changed also. The introduction or expression of love in any relationship will bring some healing to all parties involved, whether this is observable or not. It will have taught love, not fear. It will have reminded all those involved, and all those observing the loving interaction, of who we really are.

Even after we have offered the miracle of love into our relationship, the other person may remain stuck in their negative feelings. However, this love may shine a few rays of light into their very clouded belief system. Many more rays may be needed for enough darkness to dissipate so as to allow their love to shine through. But every ray is needed and none are wasted, even when their results are not observable.

If we have decided that what we want in our relationship is to have our needs met and our wounds healed, or to immerse ourselves in physical pleasuring and romantic passion, or to get revenge, or to prove the other wrong, we will make certain decisions. If, however, we decide that the goal and function of our relationships is to join more deeply and to free ourselves from our fears so that we might be able to do this, we begin to feel and act differently. We then strive to determine to what degree each response, each thought, each word, each situation, or each decision supports our successful accomplishment of our stated goal. We can then begin to change these to ones that will help us accomplish our goal of peace and joining.

In truth, we have always had the capability to choose joining, peace, and love. Frank Baum in *The Wizard of Oz* expresses this point beautifully. He reminds us that life is not what it appears to be (especially when viewed through the eyes of fear). Dorothy, longing to go "home to Kansas," where it was peaceful and loving, begs the Wizard to send her back. As they are leaving in the Wizard's balloon, she jumps out to catch her dog, Toto, who has run off. The balloon, unable to stop its ascent, flies off and leaves them. Dorothy is distraught, fearing she will never again know the happiness of home. At this point, the good witch, Glinda, appears. Dorothy tells Glinda that all she wants after all her trials in the land of Oz is to return home, where she felt loved and safe. Glinda replies, "Your ruby slippers will carry you over the desert.... If you had known their power, you could have gone back to your Aunt Em the very first day you came to this country." (L. Frank Baum, *The Wizard of Oz,* New York: Henry Holt and Company, 1988)

If we had known the power within us to create our own realities, we could have immediately returned "home where we were loved and safe" and would never have needed to go through our own personal "trials in the land of Oz." However, as Dorothy helped the Lion, the Tin Woodsman, and the Scarecrow find courage, heart, and wisdom, respectively, so are we offered many opportunities to help others on our individual journeys. And like Dorothy, when she willingly gave up her chance to return home in order to rescue Toto, our service to others can speed our return Home. We have the power within us to return to a state of grace, a state of feeling totally loved and totally safe. Only a change in our perceptions is needed to return Home. Why, we have been wearing the ruby slippers the whole time.

Our existing relationships demonstrate the most common function we assign our marriages: to get what we think we want. This new paradigm demonstrates the true function of all marriages and all relationships. This function is to teach us to love unconditionally. Though the subject of this book is marriage, these concepts can universally apply to any of our relationships, with family or friends, fellow workers or neighbors, long-term relationships or "casual" ones. I have applied the concepts to the long-term "marriage" relationships, but they apply equally to any relationship.

Actually every relationship's function is to teach us this lesson. However, this concept can be easier for us to accept in our family lives than in other areas of our lives, such as our work lives or social lives. Our biggest teachers for this lesson are usually our families, and especially our mate. It is here, in the mated relationship and the immediate family, that the teaching and learning of love often takes its most obvious and intense form. Our stuff is right in our face and it is hard (but not impossible) to avoid.

Once we have begun to accept the concept that we may be causing and creating most of the situations and relationships in our lives, we have made a major shift in our personal evolution. We have stopped mistakenly seeing ourselves as the effect and correctly begun to perceive ourselves as the cause. We have moved from victim to creator.

This is a profound and important shift, perhaps the most significant that we make in our personal and spiritual growth. A major misperception and error in thinking has been corrected. We have now begun to understand who we really are, creators of our world (actually cocreators) with limitless power and ability to create whatever we can think, feel, or imagine. All the illusions and misperceptions that came before were necessary and part of our growth process. But now, having made this correction, our growth quickens and takes on a new feel and quality. After many painful, but necessary, dead ends, we have begun a path towards Home. Once on this path, we will find our lives and relationships becoming more peaceful and fulfilling with each step.

The Basis of the Healed Relationship

Creating this healed relationship involves the understanding of several essential principles. We have already discussed how our belief system creates our reality. This is the key principle on which this book is based. Explained below are four additional principles. Understanding, though perhaps not yet believing, these additional principles is helpful in creating a healed marriage.

Principle #1: We Are Always Teaching Either Love or Fear

The following example demonstrates this principle. The event took place in a Midwestern city some time ago. A young girl was murdered by a teenage boy who lived in the neighborhood. The neighbors and the city were understandably outraged. The boy was arrested and his family was under virtual siege in their home from angry citizens, who wondered what kind of parents could raise such a child.

Soon after the murder, the parents of the young girl called a news conference. Until then, they had made no public comment concerning

the tragedy. Everyone expected anger and hostility to be justifiably lev-
eled at the boy's parents, who were still living down the street. The
news conference was to be held on the front steps of the girl's home. To
everyone's amazement, the boy's parents appeared along with the girl's
parents on the front steps. The girl's parents told the community that
they had forgiven the boy and his family, and asked everyone to do likewise. They wanted no greater pain to be heaped on this tragic situation.

This "miracle," this act of love and forgiveness, affected thousands,
perhaps millions, of people as the press carried the story. The ripples continue to affect everyone who hears of their response, as it has just affected
you. There were many possible responses that they could have chosen:
hate, condemnation, anger, scorn, etc. We would have felt all of these
were justifiable and yet all of these would have taught fear. The response
they chose taught love instead.

To demonstrate is to both teach and learn. If we are not teaching and
learning (demonstrating) love, we are teaching and learning fear. What
we believe is what we teach, both consciously and unconsciously. What
we teach then reinforces our beliefs, as all behavior reinforces the beliefs
that motivate it. In this way we are always teaching and learning and the
two cannot be separated from each other. In every situation and relationship, we must ask ourselves, "Do my responses to, and feelings about, this
person or circumstance teach love or fear?" These are the only two choices,
and that which we decide to teach, we will learn.

Though there appear to be myriad emotions, in reality there are only
two: love or fear. There are no other emotions. Fear is an emotion that
comes from our egos. Love is an emotion that is given us by God. We
need only to choose differently, from love not fear, to create differently.

Saying that there are only two emotions may at first glance appear
ludicrous. It may not be at first apparent that there are only two emotions. It is easier to understand that most positive emotions (kindness,
nurturing, consideration, loyalty, fidelity, etc.) are expressions of love.
However, it is harder to see that all negative emotions are expressions

of fear. But, if we examine each negative emotion, we will find fear at its core.

Hate is a form of the fear that we are unlovable and, therefore, we hate ourselves and project this hate onto others. Jealousy comes from the fear that we may lose something to another or that we may not be as worthy as they or that we live in a universe of limited supply. Stress comes from the fear that we do not have enough time, energy, skills, knowledge, or money or a fear that bad things may happen in our lives. Greed is from the fear that we may not have enough. Dishonesty and deceit are from the fear that we may not get what we want, if we tell the truth we may be punished if others knew of our actions or thoughts.

Anger is the thought that we have been unjustly treated and the fear this "unjust treatment" will continue to go unnoticed or unpunished. It is the attempt to make another feel guilty (fearful). Pettiness and gossip come from the fear that we are not lovable. We, therefore, must judge and belittle others to seem superior to them. Depression comes from the fear that we are not worthy or valuable or that our world will not offer us happiness, peace, and joy. Despair is the fear our unhappiness and pain will not end. Loneliness is from the fear that we will always feel alone and unconnected. All forms of attack, whether they are verbal, emotional, or physical attacks, are the outward manifestations of these fears. All these fears are a calling for love.

Principle #2: "Attacks" Are Calls for Love, Help, and Healing

Several years ago I heard a woman tell a story on the radio that was a clear demonstration of a "miracle" and its healing power, though she might not have labeled it as such. She was in a dressing room at a beach changing into her bathing suit, when she heard a mother and young daughter enter the stall next to her. They were talking and did not notice anyone else was in the bathhouse. As they began to undress, the child's bathing suit could not be found. The more they searched their bag, the more infuriated the mother became at the child for leaving the bathing suit at home. As the mother began to yell, the little girl pleaded with her mother not to hit her, anticipating the pain that must have been a common occurrence in their relationship. The child was becoming increasingly frightened.

The woman in the adjoining stall was also becoming increasingly upset and alarmed. She had been mistreated as a child and knew exactly what the young girl was experiencing. All her past anger and rage towards her parents were being triggered and directed towards this mother. She decided she must do something to stop this mistreatment, to defend this little girl, to defend herself. At first, angry thoughts and words came into her mind that might shame or frighten the woman. She wanted to attack this woman so that she would stop her attack. Then in a moment of clarity and peace she knew exactly what to do. She tapped lightly on their stall and said, in a loving and compassionate voice, "I know how difficult raising a child can be. Is there anything I can do to help?"

With this the mother audibly sighed and her anger dissolved. Surprised and spent, she replied, "No, but thanks for understanding." When she heard the mother say this and sensed the release in her voice, she too was moved by love, not only for the frightened child, but for the angry mother as well. She sensed the interchange had helped all three of them. She later saw the child and mother playing happily on the beach, the child dressed in shorts and a tee shirt.

All of this woman's fears and judgments were triggered by this interchange she was witnessing, a painful dynamic so similar to ones she had experienced in her childhood. At first she returned to the past, wanting to strike out and attack the mother, wanting to attack her own parents. Then she returned to the present, and in a moment of true clarity, offered the mother what she was calling for: love, understanding, validation, and compassion. Once it was offered, this "miracle" brought healing and forgiveness to all involved. The effects of this "miracle" have continued to touch others as they heard her story on the radio or now read it in this book. It is in this way that our miracles of love can have profound, yet unobserved, effects on people we may never know. It is in this way that our acts of unconditional love, our "miracles," can heal any situation in which it is offered. Indeed, the purpose of every situation is for this miracle to be offered and in doing so remind us of who we really are.

All emotions are related to love. We are always either extending love or asking for love. When we are loving we are extending love. When we are fearful or attacking, we are asking for love, just as this young mother was doing. Perceived from a clear level, all fears and attacks are a calling for the love we fear we will not find and/or do not deserve. Negative, fearful emotions and behavior are a calling for love that has been twisted and distorted by our fears. If we consider any unloving behavior that we have witnessed or been "subjected" to, we will find a hurt and fearful "child" desperately seeking love. The appropriate response to a brother or sister seeking love is to give them love.

Viewed from this perspective, every attack, every slight, every injustice, every betrayal is simply a disguised call for love. In this way the attack is an illusion. It is not real. Only the call for help it masks is true and real. Therefore, we can never be attacked. We can only be asking for help and love, no matter how distressing or painful the form of this call may appear. These perceived "attacks," these "disguised calls for love," are as valuable to us as are truly loving actions.

Both of these actions, the love and the call for love (attack), can bring love into our awareness. Though extension of love is experienced as more "pleasurable" than calls for love, we can always be grateful to others for offering either, no matter what the form their behavior takes. We can be grateful to the friend who hugs us or the "enemy" who attacks us. They are both offering us the opportunity to teach and learn love. Obviously this is much easier to read (and write) than to do.

Principle #3: Every Situation and Relationship Can Be Used as a Teaching Aid to Teach Love

A story is told of how Gandhi used a hate relationship to teach love. As India and Pakistan were being broken into two countries, Muslim and Hindu, there were riots in Calcutta. Muslims were killing Hindus, and Hindus were killing Muslims, and both were in a bloodbath. As the riots subsided, a Hindu man came to Gandhi, in great distress. "Mahatma," he said, "I have committed a great sin and know I must be severely punished. In the heat of a riot, I killed a young Muslim child. Now I know I must suffer the rest of my life."

Gandhi's response clearly demonstrates the ability to use even the most horrific special hate relationship to teach love. "Find another Muslim child about the same age who has been orphaned by the war," he told the Hindu man, "and raise him and love him as if he were your own son."

It is in this way that every situation, every relationship, every event, no matter how painful or "negative" it may outwardly appear, can be used to teach love. In truth that is its only function. No matter what the state of an existing relationship, no matter how barren, hopeless, or painful it may be, it can be used to teach love. In doing so it will be transformed into a healed relationship. In each situation or relationship we can ask to see it through the eyes of love. We can ask, "What would love say about this?" The answer will soon be clear.

The opportunity to pierce the illusions of our fears and see our inner Divine nature is offered to us by our relationships with others. Our salvation, our remembering who we and others are, is offered us through these relationships. Every time we judge or condemn another we have forgotten who they are and focused instead on the fearful illusions of their identity. This is true for all forms of judgment, from mild irritation to intense hate. If we have forgotten who others are, we have also thereby forgotten who we are. If we believe another to be a "flawed sinner," we believe this about ourselves. It is because of this that we can only truly know ourselves and be at peace by truly knowing, and forgiving, others. We cannot get "there" alone.

Principle #4: Luck and Punishment Play No Part in God's Plan

Several years ago I was talking with a friend of mine and he was bemoaning the pain of his third divorce. At one point, he said, "After three attempts at marriage, I'm convinced I'm either unlucky or being punished. Marriage is not for me." His perception is certainly understandable. Having "failed" three times would seem to be "proof" that future failures are likely, if not assured.

He had, however, misinterpreted the lesson. The lesson here was not that he was undeserving of a loving relationship. It was rather than he was ultimately deserving. Only his fear that he was not deserving was in the way. These painful relationships were revealing this self-destructive fear-based belief system that he was unworthy so that it could be healed. He was simply giving himself three opportunities, no matter how painful, to reveal and heal this fear and remember his total worthiness. Only this fear had caused him to create "failed" marriages.

In truth, these relationships were blessings that could have allowed him to observe his fears and discover that they were groundless. Each painful "failure" was in reality a wakeup call for him to examine how he had decided that he was not worthy of love and thus created a painful relationship. He, like everyone else, is deserving of unconditional love. We were created to love and be loved. He simply chose to misperceive the painful relationships as proof he was unworthy, instead of viewing them as opportunities to release his fears and to discover his inherent worthiness.

We were created to love and be loved.

Perhaps in no other area of our life do we feel that fate plays a dominant role as in our love life. Often by fate, we mean luck. Are we at the right time, at the right place to meet Mr. or Ms. Right? If we are, we are blessed. If not, we are condemned to a lonely, frustrating love life. We often attempt to place ourselves in environments and situations where we feel the odds will be in our favor for fate and luck to shine on us.

Often, we may have come to believe that there is a limited amount of love and lovers that we are allowed. If we lose a lover (through rejection, death, to another, etc.) we may conclude that we have just used our allotted mates and no others will be granted to us. We may have decided that even if we do find other mates, we can never love them as much as we loved our former ones. Movies, novels, and songs are full of stories of unrequited love or of people who are convinced that their mated happiness is controlled by fate or luck.

Punishment also plays no part in the plan of a loving Creator. If we feel we have been unkind or unloving in past relationships, we may feel that we will now be punished for this by being denied a loving, peaceful marriage. If we left a relationship and then later regretted leaving, we may feel that future mated happiness will be withheld from us as a punishment for not appreciating the previous relationship. However, God is always offering us joy and peace, and this is never withheld or diminished because of our past. He is not judging us for our past unloving actions but rather healing us from their effects.

Luck, either good or bad, plays no part in God's plan and, therefore, luck plays no part in our lives, which is part of His plan. To believe otherwise is to believe that we are at the effect, not the cause, of our lives. If we are at the effect of a random universe, luck plays a large part in our lives. If we are at the effect of a punitive God or universe, then rewards and punishments also play a large part in our lives. These are the commonly held views on our planet at this time, so it is understandable that we have all incorporated them into our belief system. It would be almost impossible not to do so. However, as the truth that we are the cause, not the effect, of our lives begins to reemerge, this faulty view is being challenged. We are now beginning to remember that we are creating our lives by our thoughts and emotions. We are beginning to remember that we can re-create our lives and relationships to reflect the love and peace that we have always felt was possible.

Nothing Short of a Miracle Will Work

This book can be frustrating. It is gently asking you to do the hardest thing on earth to do, to love others unconditionally. My guess is that you might have already wondered whether this is past your abilities. At times it just seems so much easier to continue with our "justified" anger and judgment and with our "well-intended" desire to correct another. In reality, it is not easier. A look at the present condition of human life in general, and our lives in particular, will testify to the pain and difficulty inherent in a life full of judgment, condemnation, anger, and revenge. There is only one avenue out of this pain, and this is unconditional love.

Sometimes this seems like such an enormous task to emotionally accomplish. Especially if others have "attacked" or hurt us, this may seem almost beyond us. And in some ways it is. It may seem that it would take a "miracle" for anyone to be able to love unconditionally. And it does! However, by "miracle" I do not mean supernatural acts performed by some deity. Rather, a "miracle" is any act or thought of unconditional love by anyone, anytime. To accomplish these acts, we can continually ask God (in whatever way we understand Him or Her) to see ourselves and others through the eyes of love. Rather than condemnation, this "miracle" offers true forgiveness. This expresses God's unconditional love through us and is the only response that can offer true healing. These "miracles" are always available to us, free for the asking.

It is easy to understand the concept of loving another unconditionally, but very difficult to actually become clear enough to do it. This book offers a few techniques that will help remove the barriers we have to attaining this lofty goal. However, I believe no one approach will work for everyone. There are many paths to the road Home. Once we have decided to find a "better way" of relating, we will immediately create, or locate the specific techniques, the particular "teaching aids," that will work for us. The answer is contained within the question and it is different for everyone. The harder part is to define and commit to a goal of deeper joining. The easier part is to determine our own path to get there. This will be made clear to us once we have committed to the goal.

There are many good tools that can help in attaining this goal. The purpose of this book is not to lead you towards any one path, but rather to define the goal. Once you have committed to the new goal, all the means you need to attain it will be provided. There are no insurmountable obstacles to a healed relationship. We set our own pace to its accomplishment through our willingness to examine and then release our fears.

Chapter 3

"And They Lived Happily Ever After"

> AUTHOR'S WARNING: This chapter may be upsetting, especially if you have been hoping that romantic love would be the key to your happiness. This chapter may cause disorientation, denial, severe disappointment, depression, resentment, and anger.

The impact that romantic illusions have on us was recently demonstrated in a story told to me by a relative. A close friend of hers was diagnosed with a form of cancer that is usually fatal. He was given six to eight months to live. Before he was diagnosed, he was going out with a woman and they were considering marriage. He had been hesitant, always wondering whether she was his "perfect mate." After the diagnosis, the woman still wanted to marry him, even though she knew he would only live a few more months. My relative visited him three months after the diagnosis, while he was recuperating in the hospital from another near fatal episode. It was clear to him and everyone he could not last much longer.

At the hospital, he discussed with my relative his continuing resistance to marrying this woman. At one point he said, "But what if I meet someone I like more, later on. Maybe then I will regret marrying her and it would not be fair to either of us." My relative, somewhat stunned by the comment, remained silent. After a few moments, he looked at her with tears in his eyes and said, "I guess that isn't going to happen." A week later they were married. Two months later he died a happily married man. This man's comment to my relative in the hospital represents the incredible power of both the promise, and the illusion, of romantic love.

In the next few chapters we are going to take a good look at how most of us developed our existing perceptions of romantic love and marriage. However, we will go farther than most books on the subject in that we will do this not only from a social, cultural, and psychological perspective, but from a spiritual one as well. You may want to read the above "author's warning" again. After going through these chapters you may never again view romantic relationships the same way. Once you see that the beautiful flowers are silk, not real flowers, it is hard to be as moved by them again. So, you have been dutifully warned. Now proceed at your own risk (of dissolving fantasies).

I am not saying that romantic love should be avoided, discarded, or altered. Romantic love is an integral component of most marriages and it plays a special purpose in their conception and growth. For most of us the "romantic spark" is an essential ingredient in any mated relationship. Though in this chapter we will be looking at the myth and promise of romantic love, I am not saying that your marriage need be devoid of all or most romantic feelings. How boring this would be.

However, if we more clearly understand this powerful human emotion, we can limit its destructive qualities and accentuate its constructive ones. Now you might be thinking that you really do not need this information because your relationship is long out of the romantic phase. You might be thinking, "Forget about being in love anymore, I am just trying to figure out how to live compatibly with this person." Though for many of us the initial romantic feelings have waned somewhat (if not totally), it is still of value to examine these feelings, as they often still strongly affect us.

When we think of marriage, we usually think of romantic love. We are seeking Mr. or Ms. Right to bring us the lifelong conjugal bliss we have always hoped to find. Indeed, romantic love, being "in love," is an exhilarating and profound human experience. It is something to be cherished when found, and then nurtured as it progresses. However, it will create less pain if it is also understood.

The romantic view of the mated relationship is rather recent in human evolution. In the past, most people viewed marriage as a practical matter or as something mandated by their parents and/or culture. Though our culture may be an exception, very few human beings on this planet have married for love or romance. The modern romantic view, which is encouraged by much of our media, from fairy tales to television, tells us that one special relationship will come along, with one special person with special attributes, and that this relationship will be our salvation, dissolving our pain and loneliness. From our earliest childhood fairy tales, to the television shows and commercials we will see tonight, romantic love has been characterized as our most precious treasure. Once found, it must be carefully guarded, for if we ever lose it, we may be banished to the wretched loneliness from which we were saved.

Most romantic stories always stop at "...and they lived happily ever after." Two people ride into the sunset, looking longingly into each other's eyes, oblivious to the rest of the world. This fantasy is presented as the perfect marital union, implying that anything less is imperfect. We are never told what it took to live together that happily. It just magically happened with no work or effort on either person's part. A perfect union between two imperfect people. Unfortunately, this ideal romantic relationship can become the model by which we measure our own mated relationships. When we do this, we will always be seeking a fantasy and, therefore, never satisfied with our reality.

What a service we could offer our children if instead of ending fairy tales with "and they lived happily ever after," we changed the ending. We could say "and they rode off into the sunset and spent their lives together helping each other let go of their fears so that they could love uncondi-tionally and be truly happy." Now that is the way to end a child's fairy tale! This would set up no false expectations nor unrealistic "ideal" rela-tionships. It would serve to remind our children that marriage is not always passion and joy, but often involves the hard work of searching out and releasing our fears, our barriers to love.

Our culture and media have inundated us with messages and images regarding marriage and romantic relationships. We may be receiving hundreds of these a day and may have been exposed to millions over our lifetime. Every billboard, every commercial, every magazine cover, every television show seems to tell us that being young and beau-tiful and in love is the highest human state. These images help form and mold our concept of what we want from our marriage. These images, however, only mirror the species' fixation on the physical body and the ego. They reflect our total misunderstanding of the true function of the mated relationship.

Over and again, we are being told that the basis for a marriage is romantic love and sexual attraction. Actually, the dominant theme of most love songs or stories is usually not the joy of romantic love, but rather its pain. Most love songs and love stories dwell on either the begin-ning of a relationship (when we are longing for our mate), or the end (when we are missing them). We have glorified the pain and the longing. It has become so ingrained in our culture's thought-forms that we have only just begun questioning its validity.

To get a feel of how great an impact these fantasies are having on our culture, take a brief look at the publishing industry. Half of all the paper-back books sold in the United States are romance novels. Half! Now I understand that many romance novels, aside from being entertaining, have done much to empower women and raise their self-esteem. But many have also done much to perpetuate an illusion that in the end does not make people happy.

Romance from a Spiritual Point of View

Now let us take a look at romantic love from a spiritual point of view. At one level, romantic love is based in our highest spiritual yearnings. It represents our desire to join again and end our loneliness and separation. It is the out-picturing of our desire for perfection, joy, and love. However, once our egos, rather than our higher nature, become involved, these impulses become distorted.

The ego (the belief system of separation) deduces that we must join with another person to end its separation and find peace and happiness. And since the ego survives on its "specialness," it must be a special relationship with a special person. It then encourages us to make this relationship our "god" and worship at its altar.

It is important that I define the word "ego" here as I will be using it throughout the book. This is kind of tricky so follow me here. By the term "ego," I am referring to our entire belief system that perceives ourselves as being separate and alone and needing to find someone or something outside ourselves in order to be "whole" and at peace. It is our entire mistaken belief system of who we are: i.e., skin-encapsulated beings, separated from God and each other. This ego was made as a substitute for our real "self" that God created, which is part of God and everyone. This definition of the ego describes our entire psyche, of which the traditional psychoanalytic use of the word "ego" is a part.

The romantic view of joining, created by our egos, presents marriage as a "special love relationship," which the ego has defined as the uninterrupted bliss of mutual admiration, physical pleasuring, and emotional harmony. The reason that any relationship constructed with this model is short-lived is that it can only exist in fantasy, not in reality. In reality, this "special love relationship" is not true love, but rather the temporary pleasure of "fulfilled" dependency. It is not real love, but rather codependency. Mix in some sexual attraction and pleasuring and you have the illusion of love hiding under the guise of real love. However, it is only the illusion.

A romantic relationship, as with all special love relationships, always gives to get. It is for getting. We give and expect to receive in return. Love, attention, fidelity, specialness, respect, trust, kindness, sex, and accessibility are offered and are expected in return. We may even see it like a "bank account," whereby if we have made certain previous deposits of affection, energy, devotion, time, helpfulness, etc., we have a right to withdraw these on demand at a later date. This "giving to get" is not real love, but a well-disguised bargain. Each person trades what the other wants in order to get what they want. "I will give you what you need, if you will give me what I need" is the ego's version of love. But it is not true unconditional love, which is union and inclusion. Rather, it is an illusion of love involving separation and exclusion that is substituted in love's place. In contrast, true love is for giving. It asks nothing in return. The experience of loving is our return payment— many times over.

We have been conditioned to think that one special person will come along to fill the gaping hole we feel inside. When we seek to fill these holes with another person, we are actually only trying to cover the holes, not fill them. Rather than healing ourselves through the often frustrating and painful work of releasing our fears, we hope that meeting the right person will somehow instantly and magically heal us. We believe the right partner will restore us to the wholeness we feel (mistakenly) we lack.

This wish for a special relationship to fulfill our needs has become even more pronounced in the modern Western world. Given the way in which our family and community relationships have fractured, we are often looking to our mates for all the support and communication that was once spread over many people (parents, grandparents, siblings, relations, friends, and neighbors). In the past, often our relatives helped with child rearing, our neighbors were supportive friends, our parents lived close by and were accessible. For many of us, that has all changed. Families are becoming more and more isolated, with only themselves to turn to. We risk becoming a culture of individuals, with little sense of commitment or connection to a larger whole. We may be looking to our mates to fill many, if not most, of our emotional and social needs.

We have been further conditioned to believe that once this special person does finally appear, we will be able to lose ourselves in them through intimacy and passion. We expect this to last a lifetime, yet fear that it will all too soon fade. This fading is unacceptable to the ego, which is oriented towards being special, and therefore better. If we, and our chosen mate, are special, then we believe we are in some way better. This belief is essential to the ego, which hates the concept that we are all equal and the same. To the ego we must be special.

After our ego has filtered our innate desires to love and join, they are almost unrecognizable. Being "in love" is not really love. It is a powerful emotion that we have been trained to interpret as love. Often it is the ecstasy of feeling (mistakenly) that our loneliness has finally come to an end, and that our joy will begin. Finally, our long night of loneliness is over. Finally, we will know the true love we have always longed for. Finally we will be at peace.

Falling in love is not a conscious act, as we can neither choose who we fall in love with, nor who falls in love with us. We often fall in love with people we do not respect or like, or with whom we have little in common. Sometimes we fall in love with people we have never actually met. Some people fall in love several times a day just watching television. The experience of being in love is usually temporary because, if you look closely at the concept of the special love relationship, you will find it is an impossibility. It is attempting to join what cannot be joined. True joining can never happen between bodies, which merely represent the ego's belief in separation. True joining only happens between minds, and all minds are always joined.

The romantic relationship does have a common outer form, which makes it appear as if we have joined together in a mutual goal. Couples flush with romantic love seem to be the epitome of "two becoming one."

However, the romantic relationship is still dominated by our individual egos. The outer form of the marriage satisfies our separate interests, but both people are in the relationship for separate, and often quite different reasons. You are in the relationship for what you can get out of it, and I am in it for what I can get. If you give me what I want and need, I will gladly give you what you want. Rather than a true joining, this is a trade, each trading for something that they think they lack.

The Impossibility of Joining Through Separation

When we are in love, everyone but our beloved is excluded from the relationship. No one else but them can clearly perceive our specialness, our true inner beauty. The special love relationship is mutually exclusive, seeking to bar all others from it. It is me and my beloved against the world. Even if no one else can see our true beauty, our beloved can, as we do theirs. It is a relationship founded on separation from everyone outside the relationship; and since peace and happiness come from seeing all people as one, therein lies its weakness and tragic flaw. We have decided joining with one special partner really is true union. No one else is needed in this union. Ironically, we are seeking union and joining through separation and isolation.

The ego is seemingly willing to share its specialness with another person, but really it is not. In truth, it is this desire to be special that keeps us apart from everyone, even from our beloved. When the romantic fervor fades, we often leave the relationship in search of the next romantic attachment. Or, if we remain in the relationship, we blame the other for having to live unhappily ever after (the special hate relationship).

However, the insanity of the ego relationship does not stop here. The special love relationship also actually excludes the two people it is attempting to join. Sound crazy? Just watch. When we are in love, we do not seek to know the reality of the other person, but rather the mutually agreed-upon fantasies both have created. We see each other at our "best," hiding from one another our fears, our insecurities, our past, our habits, our pain, our "reality." Often we feel all these unattractive parts of ourselves have magically disappeared, since we have finally met the right person. We feel wonderful and they seem wonderful. In this illusion, we are sure we have met just the right person with those special attributes we have always sought. And in doing so, they have brought out only our best. Only later, in Stage 2, does the disguise begin to unravel.

Romantic relationships do not really join two people as they really are, but rather join the fantasies of each person. The "real" person with their insecurities, their fear, their habits, their defenses, their slights and betrayals, etc., are not welcome in this relationship. We only welcome the "best" of each person. Therefore, even the two people are excluded from the union. It is a union involving the fantasies of two people. Because of this dynamic, the special love relationship must fail at its attempt to bring real union. Once again the ego's war cry of "Seek but do not find" prevails.

In this romantic illusion, emotional harmony and compatibility are valued and sought, not emotional healing. Here denial and minimizing are mistaken for peace. In a special love relationship we try to conceal our wounds from the other person and each person attempts to reveal only their "best" side to the other. The totality of who they are, including their fears and insecurities, is often hidden. During the romantic relationship, especially at the beginning, the other seems to bring out only our best. However, after the initial flush of emotions begins to fade, each person's insecurities and imperfections may begin to surface. Now we either begin to fear our "flaws" may drive our loved one away or theirs may drive us away. This fear creates deception rather than honesty. Romantic love thrives on the dishonesty and fantasy.

Romantic relationships do not really join two people as they really are, but rather join the fantasies of each person.

It is while we are under this delusional and passionate state of mind called "being in love" that we frequently make a "lifelong" decision of marriage. We perceive our beloved, ourselves, and our future life together through a vision clouded by fantasies, distortions, anticipated wish fulfillment and strong sexual urges. In this clouded state, no matter how exhilarating it may be, we are asked to wisely evaluate whether our beloved is an appropriate and compatible lifetime partner. Is it no wonder the honeymoon period is so short-lived and half the marriages end in divorce? Once we see the "real person," warts and all, we may begin to think we have married the wrong person. Perhaps we were fooled during the romantic stage when they, and we, were at our best.

In truth, we have never married the "wrong" person. Each person is in our life for a reason, never as a mistake or a punishment. We have spiritually and subconsciously chosen the perfect partner to teach us certain lessons about ourselves. They have arrived offering us the gift of understanding and healing ourselves. This does not mean that we must stay married for a lifetime. Changing the "form" of the relationship from mate to ex-mate may happen. But for as long as we believe we have married the "wrong" person, we will be unable to accept the gifts they have offered us. Our blame is in the way.

Now I know I have spent a lot of time looking at its destructive aspects, however, this is not to say that romantic love is all destructive. Falling in love serves a very important function in the progression of human growth towards more mature levels of relating. The intensity and short-lived joy of the romantic relationship may serve to create a deeply felt commitment and bond towards the other person. There are shared joys, shared pleasuring, shared experiences, shared challenges that can form a relationship "history" that can be cherished. This commitment can then become the lasting basis for the relationship after the early flush of romance has lost its glow.

We are not only intimately connected to the other, but the original prospect of bliss encourages us to continue attempting to establish this connection permanently. If it was so wonderful once, can it not be that way again? The romantic phase can create a bond which can be used as the basis for the more mature phases that follow. It also offers a spark of excitement that keeps us attracted and interested. And, needless to say, the sexual attraction assures the physical continuation of the species.

Sex: The Joining of Bodies

SEX! That magic word. It conjures up who knows what images. For each of us, it means something different. However, rather than addressing these differences, I will be looking at each again from a spiritual perspective, which, at one level, is the same for all of us. But before we begin, let me put you at ease. I am not advocating celibacy. I feel a wonderful sexual life can be a part of a healed marriage. In fact, your sexual enjoyment may become heightened as the relationship becomes more healed. So, relax.

Most special romantic relationships include a strong sexual component. Because being "in love" is inevitably sex-linked, it focuses on the body and the ego, not the spirit. The ego's home is the body; and therefore it seeks to satisfy itself through it. By doing this, we incorrectly believe we can find true union through our bodies. This is especially contradictory since our bodies represent our "illusion of separation." We are, therefore, trying to find union through separation once again. Also, we have come to view our bodies as a vehicle for our pleasuring and joining. In viewing them like this, we incorrectly assume that sex, the greatest physical pleasure, will also offer us the ultimate human experience. It will not.

Then what are our bodies for? What is their function? The question almost sounds ludicrous. But it is not, and this question must be accurately answered if we are to understand their true use. The body's true function is as a teaching aid or vehicle of communication. It can be used to reach the minds of those who still believe they are only bodies and, through our bodies, we can teach them this is not so. Now, let us dissect this sentence. What it is saying is that the true function of our bodies is to use them to communicate with other people who think they are only a body, not spirit, and remind them that they are much more than a body and an ego. We can use our bodies to remind others that they are innocent spiritual beings. And by reminding others, we remind ourselves.

In reality, our bodies are instruments our minds use until the body's usefulness is over, when it can be laid aside (death). Sometimes this usefulness is for many years, sometimes a few. During this time, when we perceive and use the body for a pleasuring vehicle or an instrument of pride or attack, we begin to believe we are a body, rather than that we have a body. When we do this, we are confusing the learning device (the body) with the goal of the curriculum (to know who we are). The learning device has mistakenly become the goal of the lesson. We think we are only a body. Our bodies are really learning instruments to be used to learn the curriculum of unconditional love. We have viewed the body as the curriculum. We have confused the means with the needs. When we do this, it blocks understanding of both. We mistakenly believe we can know peace through the body and ego.

This does not mean we must become celibate or sacrifice sexual pleasure. It only means understanding the limits and purpose of our sexual relationship. If we do this, we will not expect our body to give us something it cannot, nor will we use it for attack or power. If we are using our bodies to communicate our love with another, rather than just seeking our own pleasuring, the experience will offer a deeper sense of joining and union. However, complete joy and peace will always be experienced by us on a spiritual, not physical, level.

The true function of our body, then, is as a learning device, a communication vehicle to help awaken. Why, I can just hear pickup lines in the future: "What a beautiful communication vehicle you have. Thanks. And my learning device is rather attracted to your learning device, too. Well, then, let's get together and use them to remind each other we are not bodies. Your place or mine?"

Sex Through the Stages

Usually our sexual passion is at its height during the romantic Stage 1, especially at the beginning of this stage. As Stage 1 painfully slips into Stage 2, the sexual passion and pleasure usually lessens and may finally cease all together. As Stage 1 wanes, and Stage 2 progresses, a confusing semi-celibacy may settle over the marriage (semi-celibacy? I think I just coined a new word). This is understandable. What was new and exciting is now mundane and familiar. Someone who was near perfect is now seen as flawed. The illusion of "giving" is now dissolved, revealing the less appealing face of "getting." The promise of joining through our sexual union is seeming more and more hollow.

Now yet a new fear arises. We begin to fear that our most enjoyable sexual experiences are now in the past and the future holds only mechanical or dispirited interludes, if any at all. For a generation brought up and still fed on a continual diet of images glorifying sex, this can be very hard to accept. This fear can become so intense that it can drive us into seeking new sexual partners to provide new passionate experiences, either through divorce and remarriage or extramarital affairs. Many otherwise healthy, salvageable marriages have been broken up because one, or both, of the partners felt the desire for more sexual passion.

However, there is good news for those of us willing to continue together through the frustrating and difficult, but always rewarding, task of creating a healed relationship. As Stage 3 begins to emerge, the sexual relationship may take on a new life and spirit. The physical intimacy begins to reflect the greater emotional and spiritual intimacy that this stage offers. The lowering of walls and defenses during this stage allows for a new closeness and trust that also can manifest in the sexual relationship. The emphasis on giving is reinstilled in all parts of the relationship. The frequency and importance of sexual encounters may lessen during Stage 3. Sex is no longer needed to "prove" our caring and closeness. Nor is it needed as a release from tensions that are diminishing through our healing process. While the frequency and importance may wane, the enjoyment of these encounters may begin to grow. One day we awaken to realize that, rather than in the past, our most tender and intense sexual experiences may be in the present and future.

The Romance Fades and Stage 2 Begins

My premise is that Stage 1, the romantic, beautiful honeymoon period, must end, as all fantasies fade before the truth. Many of us hate to admit this, but our experiences and all the research on romance and marriage bears this out. I further contend that the painful Stage 2 is not "real," but rather another illusional state. However, even if a dream is only a dream, when it is a bad dream, we can still feel a lot of pain. Stage 3, the healed marriage, is the final, and only "true" stage, as only it represents our "reality" as innocent children of a loving God.

Usually Stage 2 must be passed through, much as the knight must pass through the dark forest and slay the dragon before returning home. As the bliss of Stage 1 recedes, our unhappiness begins to reappear. We may now blame this on our mate and our relationship, where in the past we may have blamed it on the lack of one. The ego's plan for finding happiness is, rather than change ourselves, to try to change external circumstances, people, and events until we find happiness (which we never do). The source of our happiness is, therefore, always perceived as something (or someone) outside of ourselves. We may think we need to find a certain mate (or leave one), get a better job or quit one, change our bodies to be thinner or fatter, own this possession or accomplish this feat. The list goes on and on.

We seek everywhere but within, thinking our happiness is just around the bend—with the next mate, the next job, the next divorce, the next leap in personal growth, etc., etc., etc. If we believe happiness is in something or someone outside of us, we must correspondingly believe that unhappiness is inside. If we believe love is outside, we must believe hatred is within. Otherwise, why are we seeking something outside ourselves?

We believe for us to have peace and happiness things outside ourselves, other people, and our circumstances must change. Everything must change but ourselves. We then use our minds to determine what must change, forgetting that it is only the mind itself that must change. When we realize that whatever we were looking for has failed to bring us peace and joy, we quickly identify yet one more thing that we hope now will. "I know I just got the relationship (job, money, possession, accomplishment, acknowledgment, etc.) I always wanted, but I only need this next thing to be happy." Until we understand this dynamic, we will constantly seek for something outside to complete ourselves rather than seeking within. Once we understand it, we will seek a better way. We will begin to search within.

The special love relationship represents another fruitless attempt to find happiness outside ourselves. The special hate relationship begins when we realize this is not going to work. In a special love relationship, emotional issues soon begin to surface after the initial honeymoon period (Stage 1). Soon the romantic feelings begin to fade, often to be replaced by feelings of blame and judgment. This is the beginning of the second stage. This conflict may lead us to seek another "perfect relationship" with a different partner, or to feel doomed to struggle "unhappily ever after," with the present mate.

Only after the honeymoon period begins to fade do the other person's flaws begin to emerge. Their insecurities and fears, their idiosyncrasies and strange habits, unloving and inattentive responses, supposedly unnoticed until now, begin to surface. We begin to fear that maybe our choice in a partner for our special relationship was not well made. We begin to wonder if they are worthy enough. Perhaps we should seek one more worthy. Also, because of the tremendous impact they have on our lives, we become much more intolerant of our mate's flaws than of those of others around us. And yet it is from these same mates that we demand the greatest acceptance of our own flaws.

Or perhaps we begin to wonder if we are worthy enough ourselves. We fear that we are unable to meet their needs, to keep their attention, to love them purely enough, to be enough. Perhaps we are too internally flawed to create a loving relationship. Whether we blame our mates or ourselves, it is usually now that the special love relationship also becomes a special hate relationship. The relationship then begins its painful swing from a special love relationship, full of total acceptance and bliss, to a special hate relationship, with its condemnation, resentment, and conflict. Many relationships get stuck here and it's not a lot of fun.

The special hate relationship often intensifies when we make a commitment to a relationship, such as when we move in together, get married, have a child, or decide to be monogamous. This painful stage is often ushered in on the wings of such a commitment. Before the commitment, the relationship was viewed in terms of its potentiality. During the honeymoon stage, we were either sure our partners could heal all our wounds and supply all our needs, or we were trying to evaluate whether they could. Once committed, all that changes. Now we have chosen our life mate. Now they had better deliver. We have placed all our eggs in their basket. This is why many people say, "We were so happy until we got married (started living together, had the baby, etc.). Then everything changed—for the worse."

The Last Illusion, the Last Attack

Now, here comes the good news and the bad news. The good news is that the special love relationship is the last illusion we seek. The bad news is that it is a very powerful illusion. Let me explain. Human life is a process of seeking fulfillment and peace, though on the surface it seldom appears so. We seek this "peace" through physical pleasuring, then possessions, then power, then belonging, and finally in self-actualizing. We think if we can just get these things, we will finally feel free and at peace. Forgetting that this peace is an inner attribute, we seek it outside ourselves. In earlier stages of spiritual development we deal with more basic illusion. We think if we own enough possessions, or receive enough applause and recognition, or control enough power, complete enough accomplishments, we will be at peace.

Forgetting that this peace is an inner attribute,
we seek it outside ourselves.

Actually to find peace, to be in a state of "at-one-ment," is the goal of all human endeavors, though this is often not immediately apparent. We want more money, so we can have peace from financial concerns. We want revenge, so we can feel free from the anger that we feel toward our perceived attackers. We want possessions because we think we will be happy once we get them. We want acknowledgment or recognition believing we will feel worthy when perceived a certain way by others. If they think we are worthy, maybe we are. We want a special love relationship, so that we can feel peace that the "hole" is finally filled. We are always searching for that experience of feeling truly at peace—a feeling that we have arrived and can finally relax.

Toward the end of this exhausting cycle of "getting and doing," or "seeking and not finding," we finally realize that we only need one thing to be happy. We only need love. That is what we have been looking for all along. We have advanced far enough in our personal evolution to understand that only love can bring happiness. However, now the ego (our belief system in separation), feeling threatened by the possibility of true joining, tells us we will find this love not from within, but rather from another separate body—in a special love relationship.

This final illusion, and maybe the most powerful, is the illusion that we will be complete through our special love relationship with another person. This may be a romantic relationship or perhaps another type of special love relationship, such as one with a child, a parent, a friend, a guru, etc. Even if our culture did not overwhelm us with this concept, we would create it ourselves, as it is the final illusion before penetrating all illusions. In reality, the culture is just reflecting back to us our own deception.

After earlier detours, we have finally realized that Love is what we have always been seeking. Soon after realizing this, the ego, sensing itself threatened by the joining that true love offers, defends itself by convincing us that we are in fact seeking love. But it is not God's love we are seeking (that is within us), but rather love from outside ourselves, the love of a special person in a special relationship. "Yes," the ego says, "you're right. We're not going to find happiness in all those other silly things we sought, but in love. I don't know why we ever thought to look anywhere else. We must have been crazy. Anyway, now let's go out and find ourselves that perfect love-mate, who will finally give us happiness."

The special relationship is, therefore, the ego's last stand and most powerful attack against God (the Love within). The ego says that it is not God that we are yearning to join with after our separation, but another person. In this way the special relationship is the ego's answer to our true "oneness," our inner Divinity. Our ego perceives this as a threat, since it offers true union. Remember, the ego is the part of our mind that believes we are separate and alone. To avoid true union, it says that only union with another can give us true peace. In our illusion, the ego actually uses all our special relationships as a weapon to keep us from God (unconditional love). By believing that we will find our happiness through others, we make them our "gods." We become idol-worshippers, at the altar of the special relationship.

So, next time you see a young couple looking deeply and romantically into each other's eyes, just walk up to them and say, "Do you two realize that your relationship is your ego's last attack on God? Do you realize that you are worshipping each other as idols and this can only lead to pain and frustration?" They will quickly thank you for saving them from the illusion and its eventual pain. They will not have to pass through Stage 2, but go directly to Stage 3 and collect $200. It works every time.

Many people, who have successfully freed themselves from other illusions, can get caught in this one for a long, long time. The world rushes to agree that the romantic love relationship is the ultimate human experience. It is very seductive. Its lure is strong and concealed behind the faulty logic of our desires and our ego. It seems reasonable that our painful loneliness can only be relieved by finding another body to be with. Though apparently reasonable, and sometimes temporarily effective, the illusion will not really work. We will once again be left with that familiar feeling of disappointment and frustration after having gotten what we thought we so dearly wanted only to find the same longings, the same hollow feeling, the same painful confusion and sense of separation.

Now remember, I am not saying that in a healed relationship there is no room for romantic feelings. You will want to put this book down right now if you think this is what I am saying. I am just saying do not make the other person and your relationship your "gods" and believe your happiness resides there. In reality, romantic love is not a basis for a healed relationship, though it is usually an essential component. A healed relationship may contain romantic feelings with its much broader context, but this romantic love is not its basis. Basing a relationship on romantic love will create a certain amount of excitement, pleasuring, and enjoyment, at least for as long as the romantic feelings continue. However, romantic love can never offer us the deep peace and sense of connectedness we seek. No matter how much we wish otherwise, no matter how alluring an intimate relationship with another person may appear, only the unconditional love of God can offer this.

We may not yet understand that this "hole" was created when we perceived ourselves separate from our Creator (the "detour into fear"). This happened when we incarnated in a physical body and mistakenly believed ourselves alone and separated from God and all others. This false perception is the cause of all our loneliness and pain. Often this is not experienced on a conscious level. It is experienced as a feeling of restlessness and longing that we try to placate with things, accomplishments, power, and people.

However, this "hole," this void, cannot be filled by another person, because another person is not what is missing. Since we have never really been separate from our Creator, nothing is really missing. It is only an illusion that something is missing. But this illusion appears real and is very painful. The special love relationship always obscures our most powerful, though unrecognized, attraction toward our Creator. His love is the only love that can truly satisfy us, because it is the only love there is. When we are expressing unconditional love towards another, we are expressing God's love. And unconditional love is the only real love we express. All other "types" of love are only illusions of love.

It is understandable that we do not as yet accept this concept. We must first understand how much of our pain is caused because we have rejected God's love. Only then will we value what we have thrown away and try to find it again. However, having arrived at this final illusion, we can be comforted in knowing that we will understand, as we have with all other detours, that this path too is only an illusion and will not give us what we thought. Having finally understood this last illusion, we will emerge as our true selves to find the joy and peace we have always sought. We are very close now, with only a few more steps needed to cross to the other side.

Also, we form "other special relationships" with people other than our mates. These include friends, relatives, coworkers, neighbors, and even strangers. All of these can be special if we think the other is the cause of our happiness or unhappiness. We may, for instance, have a special love relationship with our children in which we believe our happiness resides in them. We may always be longing for an ex-lover or parent, who either died or left. We feel that we can never be fully or totally happy without them. This is a special love relationship.

We may have a special hate relationship with a parent in which we are blaming them for our unhappiness. We may have a long-standing grudge with a neighbor or old lover or mate or even with an entire cat-egory of people (whites, blacks, Jews, Christians, foreigners, homosex-uals, homophobics, conservatives, liberals, etc.). We may be angry at the person who just cut in front of us in traffic. These are all special hate relationships. We feel (fear) our momentary or long-term unhappiness is due to them.

Also, we can have a special relationship with things or concepts. We may have a special relationship with a particular religion or spiritual path (and believe God even has a special relationship with it). We then believe everyone must believe in "our path" to find salvation and peace. We can have a special relationship with losing weight, believing that we will really be happy when we hit our "perfect" weight. We may think we need to find the perfect job, or house, or town to be happy. Or with finding the right car or bedroom set. We may have a special hate rela-tionship worth getting revenge or inflicting "deserved" punishment. We have a special relationship with whatever we idolize and make our gods. We have a special relationship with anything or anyone outside ourselves that we think will make us happy or unhappy.

Transformational experiences, in which a special relationship becomes healed, do not just occur in long-standing relationships between relatives, friends, or mates. They may occur between strangers in a relationship that lasts only a few seconds. A friend of mine told me how, in the 1970s, she was walking down a street near Central Park in New York City. It was early morning and the sidewalk was empty except for a man approaching her from the opposite direction. As they closed in on each other, she noticed that he was somewhat disheveled, in the "hippie" style of the day. My friend, who was immaculately dressed and from the "establishment," had a lot of attitudes toward these counterculture youths. As she approached, she felt her judgment and resentment grow, and she sensed he felt the same. She could feel the tension between them grow as they approached each other on that lonely sidewalk. They saw each other as enemies, forced into an encounter on the "intimacy" of a New York street.

As they got a few feet apart, a "miracle" happened. They simultaneously noticed that they were both wearing the same "peace" button. They burst out laughing, both aware of the other's judgment and yet now seeing their philosophical commonality. Each knew why the other was laughing. Each knew of their own and the other's judgments. As they passed, they looked into each other's eyes with love and humor, still laughing, aware of their own mistake at perceiving a brother or sister as an enemy. It had only taken seconds for a special hate relationship to become a healed relationship. Twenty years later, she told me this story because it was still a vivid memory of an experience of real love. Anything else she did that day, or that week, she could not remember.

So What Is God's Love, Anyway?

Perhaps this message of making nothing our "god" but God (unconditional love) was what was meant by the first commandment. The first commandment, the first thing God wanted us to know was, "You shall have no other gods before me." Why was this one concept so important that it was the first thing God wanted us to understand? Why not first tell us not to kill, enslave, or abuse others? Surely these are more serious transgressions. I remember hearing this in my Sunday school class and wondering, "Is God insecure, demanding to be first in everyone's minds?" I mean, are there support groups for Gods with ungrateful children?

Perhaps, rather than a warning from a punishing, judgmental God, it was a blessing from a loving God. Perhaps we were being told that if we think we will find joy and peace in anything other than God, in anything other than unconditional love, we will not. All other paths such as money, possessions, power, pleasuring, relationships, etc., when we make them our "gods," when we idolize them, will only lead to pain, frustration, and disappointment. Perhaps a loving Parent wanted His children to know that, first off. Perhaps he wanted to help His children avoid a lot of pain.

The premise of this chapter is a tough one to accept. It suggests that we may need to give up our hope that a loving, passionate, exciting, fun-filled special relationship will bring us lasting happiness, and accept instead that we can only find this in some as yet amorphous concept called "God's love." This does not sound like a trade-off that most of us would be willing to make. Maybe, we are thinking, we can just keep trying with the special relationship. Maybe this book is wrong and we really can find all the peace and happiness we want through our relationships. Our egos shout, "Gimme a break! I'm offering you love, passion, excitement, companionship, and instant, effortless healing. What's the other choice? Some type of love from someone or something that cannot even hold you or help with the bills. On top of that you've got to really work on yourself to receive it. With my way you just have to find the right person and presto. You tell me. Who's got the better deal?"

Actually, the ego does have the better deal. The only problem here is that the ego cannot really deliver. Probably by now you are beginning to suspect as much. Just the fact that we keep trying is an example of the triumph of hope over experience. However, the pain of our past and existing relationships may have caused us to wonder if perhaps the promises of the ego's method are unattainable. We need to examine its offer carefully.

Do we really know of anyone who has found true peace and certain happiness through their intimate relationships? The key word here is "true." We may think we know a few couples who have but, on close inspection, we may find that it is not because of the relationship that they are finding peace. What we may be perceiving as a successful love relationship may not be "real" happiness and lasting peace, but rather harmonious dependency mixed with genuine caring. The problem here is that should anything happen to the relationship (if someone dies, leaves, divorces, stops loving, etc.), the happiness and peace are also gone. The dependency becomes apparent.

Or what we think is a Stage 3 relationship may just be a well-disguised Stage 2, perhaps disguised both to the two participants as well as the outside world. How many times have you thought, "I can't believe they are breaking up. I thought they were the happiest couple I knew." Or another possibility is that what we perceive as a successful special love relationship is actually a disguised healed relationship. Consciously or unconsciously, it is the spiritual understanding and perspective of the people involved that is offering them this peace, and they also have a loving relationship.

Do we still really think our relationship will be different, that we will beat all the odds and find real peace outside ourselves in our relationship? Hopefully, after reading this chapter it will be clearer that it just does not work. No matter how much we want to find that perfect mate and perfect relationship, no matter how long held and deeply felt our certainty that when we do, we will finally be happy, it just is not going to happen that way. No way, no how!

Then comes the real question. If we are not going to find what we are searching for in our relationships, then where? We have probably already tried possessions and accomplishments and they did not work. So, what is left but a spiritual path, no matter how elusive or intangible that may be. So, maybe it is in God's love, you say, and what exactly is God's love anyway?

You do not have to have a profound transcendental experience to understand God's love. Having had few of these myself, I am always struggling to truly understand what it is I am supposed to be looking for. And no one can really tell me. Indeed, God's love cannot be communicated verbally or in writing. It can only be experienced. However, I think there are some common human experiences and feelings that may give us a true sense of what His love is.

TRANSCENDENTAL MOMENTS: There may be a few occasions in our lives where, if only for a brief moment, we have felt true peace, happiness, and oneness. In religious terms this is called "grace." It may have been triggered by a specific moving event such as a death, birth, life threatening illness, reunion with a loved one, etc. Or it may have just occurred spontaneously and for no apparent reason, or during meditation or prayer. Many people who have had near-death experiences report feeling this profound love and peace when they "died" and were released (temporarily) from their physical bodies. It cannot accurately be described, but may be experienced as profound joy, or a sense of being without a physical body, with no sense of time and space.

This is God's love expressing directly. Because of its power, it must only express directly for brief instants. If we experienced it for sustained periods, we would not be able to function on this planet, or remain in our bodies. These transcendental moments could be called "holy instants," where, for a moment, we experience the profound peace and "at-one-ment" of God's love. This is God's love experienced directly.

UNCONDITIONAL LOVE: In various relationships, again if only for brief periods, we have experienced unconditional love toward, or from, another. This is a feeling of true love not because they have finally changed, or done something that agrees with our expectations, but just for being the person they are, flaws and all. This can occur between mates, friends, parents and children, coworkers, or even between strangers. This experience may last for a moment, or may be quite extended. We may have been feeling this way toward another for many years, even a lifetime. Perhaps we have loved our child like that, or our sibling or parent. I have a best friend whom I have loved unconditionally for forty years. These are the healed relationships—the expressions of God's love manifested through human relationships.

LOVING DECISIONS: We may have observed ourselves making decisions in a more loving manner, where healing and love, rather than attack and retribution, are the desired goals. Perhaps someone has hurt us and we decide to love and forgive rather than condemn and retaliate. We may decide to be helpful in a situation we could easily have avoided. We may have decided to do a "random act of kindness." As we make these decisions, we notice that we feel more peaceful, more one with others. This is God's love expressed through our conscious choice.

A SENSE OF HOME: All of us, at one time or another, have had a sense that this world is not our true Home, that we are in some sense alien here. A memory, or feeling, haunts us as if there were a place that called us to return, a place of peace and love. Sometimes this may be a strong, persistent feeling, other times hardly felt. We avoid this feeling and occupy ourselves by keeping incessantly busy or deny the feeling exists. We seek this Home in myriad ways, but none seems to satisfy our restless minds. That is because this world is not our Home. We are only Home when we are surrounded by God's love (grace). This is our natural state and it is why we feel so restless when we are not in it. No other love will satisfy us because there is no other love. This is God's love expressed directly and continually. When we are Home, we will no longer "dream" ourselves as separate and alone.

When the Romance Ends, the True Marriage Begins

Many of us feel that when we fall out of love, the relationship is over. The choices seem to be to remain in the relationship "unhappily ever after," or leave the relationship to seek a better, purer special relationship. What we are failing to understand in this scenario is that it is after we have "fallen out of love" that the "real" relationship can often begin. We are finished with the fantasies and now confront the reality of the other person. Hopefully, the initial "in love" period has created a commitment from where real love can begin. The real "love" relationship, one in which we are truly concerned with the other person's spiritual growth, often begins when we are falling out of love. Now real love can enter a relationship that is becoming increasingly free of fantasies and illusions, neurotic needs, unrealistic expectations, and unarticulated fears.

If we begin to accept that no special relationship or person will ever fill this void, we may feel a profound sense of disappointment, even anger. The ego has been reassuring us for a long time that a special person would perform this role. We have been looking forward to their arrival, or have been trying so hard with our existing mate. The promises and potentials of a special relationship have become a big part of our lives, perhaps the dominant part. We worship at that altar daily.

The ego has been telling us that everything will be wonderful when we finally get the relationship we want.

Once we begin to realize how much we have invested in our special relationships, we may become appalled. There may be an understandable tendency to condemn and judge ourselves when the insanity of our ego begins to emerge. As the illusions of the special relationship become clear, we wonder how we could be so selfish, so insecure, so unconscious, so deluded. We begin to wonder if the distance between our present level of awareness and the clarity we seek is so great as to be insurmountable in the remainder of our lifetime. When these emotions emerge we need to be gentle and compassionate with ourselves. The illusions and unconsciousness of the planet have prevailed for many thousands of years. The veil has been pulled very tight and it will take some time to lift.

However, it is only a thin gauze veil, ready to dissolve at the slightest touch of truth. Where we are now, collectively and individually, is exactly where we need to be. Every relationship we have been in was with the right person, no matter how "wrong" it seemed. Everything we have experienced in the past, no matter how insane it may now appear, is exactly what we needed to experience. Every life situation is necessary to make us aware of what we need to heal.

*Every life situation is necessary to make us aware
of what we need to heal.*

Though lasting peace, love, and happiness can only come from our relationship with our Creator, this does not exclude us from having a mate and a wonderful, loving, and intimate relationship. Many people resist embarking on a true spiritual search, as they mistakenly believe that in seeking a relationship with the Divine, they must sacrifice certain relationships, feelings, possessions, and experiences they really want.

We have come to relate God and spirituality with the concept of sacrifice, and perhaps even celibacy, poverty, and a monastic life. We will never be asked to sacrifice anything that would bring us peace. And peace is all we really want.

To understand and accept that the hole we feel inside can only be filled by God (because the illusory separation from Him created it) does not mean that we should, therefore, repress our desire for or cease our striving to create a wonderful mated relationship. Only a cruel God would allow His children to have a deep longing that could never be fulfilled. It only means that we are not making it our "god" and putting these relationships before Him. Rather, we can offer our relationships to God to be used to express His love for all. God will not deprive us of our relationships. He will transform them and restore them to their true function—to teach unconditional love.

Chapter 4

Reinterpreting the Early Years

My wife, Julia, and I recently had an argument that, as we later dissected it, revealed to us the overbearing presence of our childhood programming. Actually it was the same argument that we have been having over the many years of our marriage. For many years my arguments with Julia followed the same pattern. I would do something that she would interpret as my not listening to her. Perhaps I would forget to do a small favor she had requested or forget to mention to her some detail of a planned arrangement or other logistical detail. She would interpret this "not listening" as not honoring her or valuing her. In reacting to this, she would criticize me, usually with irritation or anger. Since there was some truth to what she was saying, I chose to interpret her attack as an indication that I was in some way "flawed" for not being "perfect" enough. I assumed the anger was the tip of the iceberg, when in reality it was most of the iceberg. However, usually these "core arguments" most of us have been having for years in our relationship are "accurate" in the sense that the unconscious behavior our mates have been trying to get us to look at is indeed there.

As we considered our past, it became clear to both of us that these issues are the ones we have been working with since our childhood. Julia was raised in a family where her family and her siblings often did not value her or her thinking. They often ignored or ridiculed her. Hence, she came to believe that no one really listened to her. Her main fear in a relationship is that someone will not listen to her, that they will not value her. I was raised in a home where it seemed that no matter how well I did anything, it was never enough to really attract my parents' attention and interest in me as a person. Their attention was always more centered on their own lives. Hence, I felt that I could never do enough, I could never be "perfect enough" to win their attention and interest. My main fear is that I am never enough. In our relationship, we were both trying to prove our "shadow figures" wrong.

Though these shadow figures include people from our childhood who often made us feel loved and safe, the most dominant and obvious shadow figures are people who treated us harshly or indifferently and did not give us the love we needed. They are usually our parents, siblings, and early caregivers. Also, they are past lovers, teachers, friends, employers, etc. Given that even from a young age we have also been seeking perfect love (Heaven), and since no one has ever been able to give this to us, at some level everyone in our past has denied us what we truly wanted. In this way almost everyone from our past is a shadow figure, though some obviously affect us much more than others.

However, usually the dominant shadow figures are those that have had a negative effect on our sense of being lovable. They are people from whom we never felt we received the love, attention, and acceptance that we very much wanted from them. They may have even treated us, for the most part, with kindness and caring, but we may not have felt we were loved unconditionally. We then go through life, and our marriages, desperately trying to get from others the love, attention, caring, validation, etc., that we believed they denied us. We will continue to do this until we understand this dynamic and make peace with our shadow figures.

Julia was trying to prove not only to me but her mother and siblings as well that she was of value by getting me to value her and listen to her. I was trying to prove to her and my parents that I was enough by getting

Julia to acknowledge it. Both of us really feared that we would react towards each other as our shadow figures had. We were both trying to change the past by creating a different outcome in the present. We were both trying to prove to our shadow figures that we did deserve love and attention by getting our present mate to give us this. (In fact, at some level, I am probably writing this book to prove to my shadow figures that I am enough. But all my mother can say is, "So what the heck do you know about marriage that you can write a book about it. Ask me, I was married to your father for forty-five years. Now I could write that book." Ah, there is just no cheese at the end of that tunnel.)

This example demonstrates how we develop our belief system regarding marriage. We have already discussed how this belief system is creating our mated relationship or our lack of one. We have also examined how our romantic fantasies were created by our belief that our happiness is to be found in someone or something outside ourselves. We have observed how the special love relationship keeps us from relating to the "real" person and demands that we relate to a romantic fantasy of them instead.

Aside from the inherent fantasy of the romantic love relationship, the special relationship is rooted deeply in our past. Now I know this is nothing new to you. We have been told for years about the tremendous effect our past, especially our childhood, has on our marriage. But remember we will now be looking at this from a spiritual as well as psychological perspective, so stay with me.

Our relationships are rooted so deeply in our past that it prohibits us from really being in the present. It does this in such a subtle, yet powerful, way. Often we are not really relating to our existing partner or spouse, but rather to a host of images of people from our past. Because of this dynamic, we go through life feeling very much wounded and cheated by these "less than perfect" relationships. We feel wounded by their past disappointments and pains, angered about past abuses and attacks, insulted by slights and injustices, injured by attacks and betrayals. We feel that we were unfairly judged and found wanting by those shadow figures and, therefore, they denied us their unconditional love. At times we fear that they may have been justified in withholding their love from us. Other times we feel this was unfair and cruel. Now we very much want to change the past so that we can prove to ourselves, others, and especially our shadow figures that we did deserve their unconditional love. We hope to restore our wounded self-esteem by changing the past through our present relationships.

We believe that if we can only find someone who will love and accept us unconditionally, all the pain of our past will disappear. However, though we think we are searching for someone to love us perfectly, instead we often create relationships where the other is treating us very similarly to the way our dominant shadow figure(s) treated us. Instead of loving us unconditionally, they love us with the same conditional love we experienced in our childhood.

We believe that if we can prove our worthiness to our existing partner it will prove it to the shadow figures of our past as well. If our mate will only love us unconditionally, it will prove to everyone that we always deserved it. We will have somehow changed our past relationships by changing our present one. This impossibility prevents us from truly relating, in the present, to our mates. Often we are desperately trying to get the approval and love of our mate (and others), mistakenly believing we need this to feel truly worthy. Having been denied this from our shadow figures, we have understandably concluded that we must get this from their "substitutes." We have forgotten that our peace, our happiness, our sense of self-worth are all attributes within us. They are not gifts or rewards granted to us by others and, therefore, under their control. We do not need the approval or love of any other person to be happy and at peace. Peace and happiness are always available to us no matter what the external circumstances of our life might be. We only need to remove our barriers, our fears, for grace to manifest in our life.

Since we know that we cannot actually change the past, we form relationships that resemble our past relationships. We hope we can change our past by reenacting our past relationship in the present, but this time with a different outcome. This time we hope that we will be loved, valued, and respected. This time we hope that someone will finally see our specialness, our inner beauty, and true worth. This time, in the present, we will finally show all the shadow figures from our past that they were wrong about us. When we discover that this does not work, we may blame our present partners for rage we feel towards all our shadow figures.

In many ways we know this to be true in our own relationships and in relationships we have observed. How often have we noticed someone marrying a person very similar to their mother or father? Often an adult child of an alcoholic will marry an alcoholic. An abused child will marry an abusive spouse. A person who had an inattentive parent will marry someone who is emotionally unavailable. A child with a critical parent marries a judgmental spouse. We tend to create mates who will hurt us in the same way we perceive our parents as having hurt us. Also, our open wounds may cause us to respond to almost anyone with the same painful responses of our past, no matter how they are really treating us. This reopening of the same wound gives us yet another chance for it to be healed.

Or perhaps we just notice ourselves and our mates overreacting to situations due to our past conditioning. We have areas where we are overly sensitive or touchy and we react inappropriately as we are again responding to many past wounds, not to the present situation. How many times have we wanted to tell our mate, "I'm not the one who did that to you. It was your parent(s). Why are you attacking me?" In reality we are often choosing a mate with similar "faults" as our parents in order that we may have yet another chance to heal our wounds. Romantic love may serve to anesthetize us during this healing process.

In all of our relationships we are trying to "correct" the past by re-creating it in our present relationship. In this way we are actually seeking to take vengeance on our past relationships by seeking this vengeance in our present one. Often this is occurring on an unconscious level. We may not be actually thinking about the past, but it may still be dictating our behavior and choices. We have created a present fantasy relationship in a futile attempt to seek retribution for the past. However, in many ways this dynamic can be welcomed, and not dreaded, as it supports the true function of the relationship. Our relationships will continually reveal to us our wounds, our barriers to joining and love, so that we (not our mate or our relationship) may heal them. As we do this, we will begin to love ourselves and others unconditionally. This then restores to the union its true function.

In addition to realizing how impossible it is to change the past in the present, it is also erroneous to believe that we really need anyone's validation in any part of our lives in order to feel that we are lovable. However, we have been programmed to believe this from our early interactions with our shadow figures. Now we are our own programmers and can change this conditioning. It only takes an understanding that the only validation we ever need is from our Creator and He offers this to us constantly and consistently. We do not need to do anything, or be any certain way, to receive this. We only need to accept our inherent value as an innocent child of the Creator. As we do this, our "planetary inferiority complex" will end.

Making Peace with Our Shadow Figures

As we observe this train of thought, we can begin to observe its insanity. In a special love or hate relationship we are in essence relating to no one. We are relating to romantic fantasies and shadow figures, both past and present. However, to the ego, whose existence is built on the past and fantasies, this thought system is essential, and though not rational, makes perfect sense for its survival. It will defend it at all costs. The ego is threatened by a healed relationship that exists in the eternal "now." It has no place in such a relationship.

We can begin to release ourselves from the grasp of this faulty belief system by both understanding that we cannot change the past and that we have misinterpreted it anyway. We are not in pain because of the love others did not give us in the past, but rather because of the love we are not giving ourselves in the present. It is not the past that we can or need to change, but rather our present thinking. Though we have no possibility of changing the past, we do have total ability and power to change our present thinking and, thereby, our belief system. By doing this we can "reinterpret" our past, rewrite history, if you will, so as to be perceived from a more compassionate and clearer perspective. However, we will resist doing this if we still feel there is something to be gained, some purpose to be fulfilled, by hanging onto the pain of the past. We will hold onto it if we feel there is still some way we can change it. We must come to realize that there is nothing we gain from holding onto our pain.

What is the past? We believe that our past is a series of clearly understood events that are accurately catalogued and recorded in our memory and brain. We base much of our present behavior on this "accurate storehouse of knowledge and experience." We believe this to be our "wisdom," which will help us avoid pain in the future. In reality, our "past" is more our interpretations and responses to the events as we perceived them. We believe we have accurately interpreted these events and the motivation of others involved in them. However, the vividness of our recollections and the impact we have allowed them to have in our lives is a function of our perceptions of certain events and how we chose to respond to them.

Our understanding of the past is not based on the "reality" of the events nor on our clear understanding of them. It is all based on our perceptions. And these perceptions were not those of a secure, clear-thinking, mature adult, but rather often they were the perceptions of an immature wounded child. If a very upset seven-year-old came to us and explained what had just happened to them, would we automatically assume that they were interpreting events with total accuracy? Who can trust the faulty memories and perceptions of a wounded child to interpret the past and to dictate present behavior? No one, we say. But we all do. Though the events can never be changed, or even accurately recalled, our perceptions of them can always be altered in the present. In this way the past will no longer dictate our future.

It is understandable and inevitable that during this period we will want to blame the unloving attitudes and actions of our shadow figures for our pain. This is a stage we must pass through. However, our process and healing is not complete until we no longer blame them. The goal during this "blaming stage" should not be to justify our anger and blame and "prove" the other wrong. Rather, our goal should be to recognize it, fully experience it, and then release it. Until then, we are still misinterpreting their unloving behavior as "personal attacks," rather than "generic" calls for love, healing, and validation. We are still misinterpreting the pain we felt as something inherent in the "attack" rather than as something we "chose." We are still misinterpreting the opportunity for growth as a negative event that should never have occurred.

There is nothing to do about the past but correct our perceptions of it and then let it go. We do this by reinterpreting the personal "attacks" as well disguised calls for love and healing. We do this by understanding that we "chose" to perceive certain incidents in our past as negative, painful events. Given the existing thinking of the world, it is understandable that we would do this. There is so little clarity out there to offer us another interpretation, another perception. Being the victim is a central component of the thought-forms of the species.

However, we can now choose differently. We do this by choosing to dwell on only the love, not the pain. Only the love was real. This is selective forgetting. All else, the slights, the indifferences, the injustices, the abuses, the attacks, were illusions. They were illusions because they were calls for help and healing grotesquely masquerading as "attacks." It is understandable that we misperceived them. They are so well hidden. However, once reinterpreted through the eyes of love, we can see that every loving thought is true. Everything else is an appeal for healing and help, regardless of the form it takes.

Every loving thought is true.
Everything else is an appeal for healing and help,
regardless of the form it takes.

We must finally come to realize that we are given the parents, care-givers, siblings, and experiences that are best able to foster within us the attributes and qualities we need to develop during our lifetime. Because we have interpreted many of the people and events as "painful" and want to blame our unhappiness on them, this can understandably be very hard to accept. The ego assures us that someone, other than ourselves, is to blame for our pain and that someone should be punished, or at least made to acknowledge their blame. The ego then forms a "special hate relationship" where another is perceived as responsible for our unhappiness and pain.

Each person was, and is, in our life because they offered us the great-est potential for learning and teaching unconditional love. We never know what traits or strengths are developed within us by pushing against what we often consider unloving or hurtful attributes of our shadow figures. Perhaps an overbearing parent teaches us to assert ourselves or an inattentive one teaches us greater independence. Perhaps a bitter parent teaches us compassion and a depressed one teaches us to take control of our lives. No matter how painful they may seem in our reflection, all our childhood experiences can be transformed into our greatest emotional and spiritual growth.

An example of how the "benefits" of a painful childhood can develop certain positive qualities in our lives can be seen in the life of Abraham Maslow. Maslow was a brilliant psychologist who studied the ability of people to "self-actualize," to make the most out of one's life. He said that it was witnessing his mother's bitterness, her stinginess, her meanness that created within him the absolute resolve to help determine how to bring out the best in people. Unfortunately, he never understood that it was just this background that enabled and empowered him to do his life's work. At the time of his death, he had not understood or healed his relationship with his mother.

Even the most painful childhoods offer us tremendous spiritual value. If someone is abused during childhood and then later in life is able to forgive the abuser, they have made great strides in overcoming their feelings to counterattack and condemn. They have learned to respond by offering love. They have learned true forgiveness and can offer this throughout their lives, and more easily in less intense relationships. This forgiveness does not mean that they have learned to "like" the other person nor to want to be physically near them. Nor does it mean they now love them as they have always wanted to love a mother or father or sibling. It simply means that they have understood their abusive behavior as a call for love by the other. The call came in a convoluted form over which the other had little control, given their existing state of awareness. Just as we are, they were doing the best they could.

As we begin to forgive our shadow figures, we will understand that we were never unjustly treated by them. They had forgotten who they were, just as we have forgotten who we are. Any unloving actions on their part were simply their call for love in a convoluted form. It was a form of fear and, therefore, not real. We can choose to perceive it differently, and thereby choose to reclaim our peace. We can begin to observe our participation in the pain by, understandably, interpreting the events as "painful." We can then begin remembering only the love from our past, as only love is real.

The "Real" Shadow Figure

So, rather than relating to the mate in front of us, we are relating to no one, only romantic fantasies and shadow figures from our past. But the power of the ego to deceive and twist reality does not stop at this level. There is one level that brings to focus the essence of the ego's attack on God. Remember that the ego is wedded to separation and God represents union. In this way God is our ultimate shadow figure. It is God that the ego is mad at and attacking. The lesser shadow figures are only symbols of Him.

Since this is not happening at a conscious level, it would be easy to dismiss this concept as faulty. God, the ultimate shadow figure! It almost sounds absurd. The ego is the part of our mind that wants us to be special, that demands that we be special. This specialness is more than just being different from everyone else. It really means that we are better. We do not want to feel that we are the same as everyone, equal to them, no better, no worse. The ego tells us that we must be special and, therefore, better. We want to feel God has made us special and loves us more than most.

We were at peace in the Garden until we asked God to make us special (better) and we began to judge. Then we lost our peace. We were banished from the Garden. We were asking God to do something that He is incapable of doing, to love some of His children more than others. He loves all His children completely, equally, impartially. Only a cruel Father would condemn us to the pain of separation through specialness. We asked of Him what only an unloving father would do, love some children more than others. Having then begun to view Him as being able to love some more than others, we began to fear Him. We began to fear that, given our "flaws and sins," perhaps He would love us less, perhaps He would even stop loving us. Our peace was then shattered. The Garden of Eden was lost.

The ego has a desire to be different and special. It wants to be God's favorite, to be loved more by Him than others. However, God has not given us the pain of separation through specialness, but rather the joy and peace of union. At a deep level we know that God has not made us special and our ego feels very threatened by that since its entire existence is based on specialness and separation. In fact, the ego was created as our answer to God's inability, which we interpret as His refusal, to make us special.

In our "dream" (life on earth) we create the ego which knows we are very special indeed. The ego then conspires to create a special love relationship in which the other person will swap their belief in our specialness for our belief in theirs. This is not a true relationship, but rather a bargain. In this way we both can prove God wrong. It is in this way that God is the ultimate shadow figure, for it is really Him that we want to prove wrong about us. It is to Him that we want to prove our specialness.

It is time we relinquished our attack on our Creator. We could never have "proven Him wrong" and if we did, the victory of being special would have only brought us more pain, isolation, and loneliness. Understanding this, God has protected us from our own insane desire to be special. He offers us only peace and joy. We have not hurt or angered Him by our attack. We do not need to be ashamed of our attack on Him. It was part of our journey Home. Our attack on Him has not disturbed His eternal peace. As in the parable of the prodigal son, He waits for us with loving, open arms. We will understand that we deserve unconditional love when we understand that everyone is equally deserving of His love.

Chapter 5

Adolescence: Solidifying the Illusion

I grew up in Atlanta from 1948 to 1965. Over that time, I had the same group of friends. There was very little change in our community during our childhood years of the '50s and early '60s. We all went to the same elementary and high schools. On weekends we went to the community center and joined youth groups and spent our summers at the country clubs or at one of the camps. It was a very stable, and yet insulated, community.

In our preschool and early elementary years we all played together, spent the night together, went to the club or camp together, and did all the things young children do before their forming egos begin to draw them apart. However, in the time from around eleven to sixteen years old we began to define ourselves in regard to our appeal to the opposite sex. Strata began to appear for both the boys and girls.

For a male, your ranking with the girls really depended on your physical looks, athletic prowess, and air of confidence. For a female, your ranking was judged by your physical appearance, air of confidence, and popularity with other girls. Scholastic achievement was an added bonus, but not required for high ranking. However, poor grades definitely lowered your ranking.

Though all of this was unspoken, it was there. There were really three different strata. There was the ranking of the top few "most desirable" girls and boys who were the most popular. They were the ones who were the most watched and talked about. They always had lots of dates to the teenage parties. They tended to have romances with each other, as the rest of us felt unworthy to pursue any "crushes" we might have on them. These were the "beautiful people," destined for great accomplishments, exciting lives, and passionate romances. In the middle was a large group of "just plain folks." They did not particularly excel in any of the "desirability factors," but they had no tragic "flaws" that made them "undesirable." They tended to have romances with each other, get along well with the group, and perhaps be a little jealous of the few stars. Finally, there were a few who, either because of a physical appearance concern or an emotional problem, tended to be left out of the early romances and began to perceive themselves as undesirable by the opposite sex. Maybe they were somewhat overweight, had bad acne, or were a little "homely." Perhaps it was not something physical, but rather emotional. They might have had very low self-esteem or poor communication skills or overt aggression.

I was comfortably in the middle group. Neither my looks nor my athletic prowess could propel me into the upper echelon. Though I desired to be in that elite circle, I accepted my fate as something beyond my control. My genes, which had blessed me with neither profound physical attractiveness nor obviously athletic skills, had doomed me to a life in the "unnoticed sea of mediocrity." It was from within this framework that I began to make certain decisions in regards to myself, my attractiveness to the opposite sex, and my eventual mating.

An incident occurred that crystallized this thinking and affected my relationships for years. This event did not cause my perceptions of myself, but rather became an internal symbol for my already developing belief system. When I was thirteen or fourteen I developed a very strong crush on a girl named Carol. Not only was she in the "top echelon," she was the "crème de la crème": beautiful, confident, smart, popular, and poised. She was way out of my league and I knew it. She had no steady boyfriend and I knew of none of my friends who were planning to "make a move" on her as most, like me, felt she was unapproachable. But I was stricken and young love pushes us out of our comfort zones.

After months of building my confidence and looking for any sign that she might even know I was alive, I decided that at the next party I was going to ask her to dance, *slow dance!* And while dancing I was going to ask her to the "J" party, one of the few and first "dated" affairs. In those days, asking someone to slow dance was the same as declaring your love and asking them to the "J" party was like asking them to marry you and spend the rest of your lives together. It was a brazen and bold move on my part, but my love-struck desire drove me on.

Finally the night came. It was a party for our group at someone's house. I remember it was the night of the Liston-Patterson prizefight, so the boys spent a lot of time watching the fight and showing off their knowledge of prizefighting (which amounted to knowing who was Liston and who was Patterson). All night long I let Johnny Mathis song after Johnny Mathis song go by, unable to muster my courage for my long anticipated move. How I feared rejection. What if I asked her to dance and she kind of rolled her eyes like, "Oh God! I guess I have to," and everybody saw that? What humiliation! I would be subtly but harshly rebuked. After all, who was I to think that I could date such a star?

It was getting late. There were only a few dances left. I was watching the fight as my internal turmoil made me bad company for the night. Then I heard it, "The Twelfth of Never," my favorite Mathis song and probably the last dance of the night. Here was my sign! My favorite song, the last song. With renewed courage I got up and went into the dance room to find my love and begin our lifetime of bliss. As I scanned the room a sight greeted me that crushed my dream, destroyed our marriage before it even began, and put me back in my place once and for all.

There was Carol walking across the dance floor with George *and they were holding hands!* George was a definite "first stringer," one of the best athletes, good looking, and arrogant. What an unbeatable combination for a thirteen-year-old girl. And if they were holding hands, going steady was only weeks away. And soon after that marriage and children and no further opportunities for our lifetime together. There was no hope. My months of dreaming and hoping came to a shattering halt on that lonely dance floor while Johnny Mathis crooned romantically, but now sadly, in the background.

At one level, it was just a typical adolescent dilemma that most of us have experienced in one form or another. However, on another level it was a profound experience that symbolized and catalyzed an attitude I had begun to adopt in regards to myself and the opposite sex. This attitude, this belief system would affect my relationships for the next twenty years. During this period I decided that any woman I truly cared for was out of my league and I could only be with someone who I did not care that much for. I only wanted women who did not appear to want me. This "new" belief system regarding myself as a mate was connected to my relationship with my loving but inattentive parents. From them I had felt that though I was lovable, I was not special or important. I then assumed this role in my early romantic relationships. There is a continuous unbroken stream of our developing belief systems, from birth to death. During adolescence it usually begins to express itself on a new tangent—our beliefs about our possibilities in our mated relationships.

The incident with Carol and George further confirmed that should I ever desire a relationship with a woman that I deeply loved, a better man would take her away. I became fearful of another "George." I feared I was not "enough" to keep the attention of a woman I loved. This was the view of mated relationships that I began to form during those sometimes painful but exciting years of adolescence.

For the rest of my youth and into my early adulthood I created relationships based on these early decisions. The women who loved me, I did not want. The women I loved, I did not believe loved me (even if in reality they did). Even if I fell in love with a woman, as soon as she returned the feelings I realized she must not be so wonderful after all or why would she care about me? After all, no wonderful woman would really be attracted to me (or as Groucho Marx once said, "Why would I want to join a club that would have me as a member?"). If I was in a relationship with someone I truly desired, I began sabotaging it as I was waiting for the "better man" to come and carry her away on his white stallion, as I waved forlornly goodbye.

I was creating my relationships from my innermost thoughts and feelings, from my complex and faulty belief system. It was law, as dependable and inescapable as the law of gravity or magnetism. I was the "cause" of my love life, but I thought I was at the "effect" of my genetic and social bad luck. These decisions, this way of viewing my relationships, became such a part of my thinking and feeling that it almost became internally unremarkable and unnoticeable to me. It was only years later that I started to articulate and examine these decisions and concepts and began to release them as faulty and inappropriate. I realized that in reality there are no levels, no tiers, no strata. We are all the same beings of total beauty and love. We are all totally lovable, but we are molded and masked by our fears of being unlovable and flawed. We are all deserving of a loving, mated relationship. We only need to release these fears to create loving and peaceful relationships.

Refining the Belief System

Adolescence is usually that dynamic time of our lives when the terms "sex" and "marriage" take on a special and mysterious meaning. It is during this time that the biological, social, cultural, and hormonal urge to be in a mated relationship first begins to bud. And like the budding of any plant, its future growth is often affected by the conditions surrounding its initial budding. Often the image we create during this period of ourselves as a mate will persist long into adulthood, perhaps for a lifetime.

It is really during adolescence that the concept of a lifetime relationship with another person becomes important to us. It is also during this period that the mating and courtship rituals begin in earnest. It is often during adolescence that we make profound, but often unarticulated and inappropriate, decisions concerning ourselves and our role and our possibilities in a mated relationship. During this period our belief system then becomes more defined and solidified. It may be valuable to spend some time recalling our early infatuations, flirtations, and romances to determine what conclusions and beliefs these may have engendered in us.

It may be valuable to spend some time recalling our early infatuations, flirtations, and romances to determine what conclusions and beliefs these may have engendered in us.

In our feelings about our mated relationships, we can usually look at the romantic experiences we had during adolescence to determine some decisions we made in regards to ourselves in this area. Though we often tend to make light of early romances and "puppy loves," the roots of many of our problems or successes in our adult mated relationships may have begun here. During adolescence we create yet more shadow figures. Those early rejections or losses can be as painful as many in adult life and the impact on us just as great. Though the roots of our feelings about ourselves extend farther back to our early childhood, they often begin to differentiate and become more specific during adolescence.

Few of us escaped that period without some type of "damage," all of which is repairable. If we experienced early rejections, we may have decided that once someone really gets to know us they will discover our inner "flaws" and no longer want to be with us. If we "lost our love" to another, we may feel that we will lose our mate to a better person or that they will always be looking for someone else. If we were romantically overlooked or ignored during adolescence, we may have incorrectly concluded that we have little appeal to potential mates. This may have made us feel undesirable and unattractive. In contrast, if we were very sought after, we may have decided that people only desire us for our outward appearance, not for who we really are. If we were very popular, we may have become very identified with our body and ego. We may have become addicted to romance or the attention of others.

Usually by the end of adolescence we have established a picture of ourselves with regard to our romantic relationships. Though this picture will alter as we grow, it often provides the basis for our future relationships. We may have decided how much joy or pain, love or rejection, peace or anguish these types of relationships have to offer us. It is important that we recall the feelings we had about ourselves during this period and understand the decisions these feelings cause us to make. It is of value to take an honest inventory of the conclusions we reached during adolescence about ourselves as a mate and examine to what degree they are still affecting us.

We usually leave adolescence with a complex and faulty view of mated relationships and our possibilities and potential in this area of our lives. Actually, there may be several conflicting views. We may have a dream of a loving, supportive, and happy marriage. In contrast to this may be images created by our fears that we will never find, deserve, or create this wonderful relationship. We may fear that we will always feel alone, even if we are mated. The relationships we create will then reflect this contradiction, with the relationship taking on the general tone of the dominant thoughts and fears.

We then take this view into our adult relationships. Our previous adult relationships also have a tremendous effect on our present attitudes regarding our mated relationship (or lack of one). We may have mistakenly interpreted any pain in these past relationships as proof that either we or the other person was in some way flawed or unlovable. This may have led to a further generalization that we cannot (or will not) have a happy mated relationship. All these faulty misconceptions must be corrected before our relationships will start to express the love and peace that we have so long desired and always deserved.

We may find that the romantic relationships we had as adults follow a certain pattern. This is understandable as we have now made specific decisions of how we are in these types of relationships. We have formed a picture of ourselves and our relationships and we proceed to paint this picture on the empty canvas of each new relationship. We have all seen ourselves or others create several similar relationships and then bemoan, "Why are all men/women like this?" They have decided that since they seem to get involved with the same type of person continually, that most people must be like that or that they just have very bad judgment or bad luck. They do not yet recognize that they are drawing a certain type of person and relationship to them based on their belief systems.

Though the possibilities and expressions are endless, there are certain common patterns in relationships. We may have decided that we can never really have the relationship we want. We then go out and create relationships with people we are not really attracted to or with people who cannot have, or do not want, a committed relationship with us. We may have decided that all relationships eventually end as people come too close or discover our tragic flaws. We then sabotage our relationship when they have run their allotted timespan. We may have experienced great pain in the past when a relationship ended, and have decided not to risk that pain again. We then decide to end the relationship once we begin to feel we are vulnerable to being hurt.

We may fear that people are only attracted to us on a sexual level and they will leave once this attraction has faded. We then create relationships based primarily on sexual attraction, fearing we are unattractive in other areas. We may have decided that others are always more appealing and "better" than us, so we create relationships in which the other person leaves us for the "better" person. We may have decided that there is only one potential mate, perfect and flawless, who will love us absolutely and constantly. We then compare every partner and relationship to this unrealistic image. We go from relationship to relationship constantly seeking the perfect one.

As we progress in our lives, we can gather more shadow figures around us that crowd in between ourselves and our mates (and others). Some of these shadow figures may even be people we perceived as rejecting us in earlier romances. These may include early loves when we were still youths. We may still be unconsciously trying to prove their assessment of us as "undesirable and unlovable" wrong. A stroll through our past in our minds may uncover if this is true for us. We can let go of the past by remembering that our pain is not caused by the love we did not receive from others in the past, but rather from the love we are not giving ourselves in the present. It is this belief that we are not lovable, our forgetting of our inherent worthiness of deserving love in all forms, that created our past and present painful relationships. It is through our love, and our healed self-esteem, that we will create the loving marriage we have always sought and always deserved.

Chapter 6

Bypassing Our Pain:
An Exercise in Futility

A friend of mine was recently telling me about a relationship she had many years ago. The man she was involved with was very troubled and had an alcohol problem. Many times she tried to "rescue" him and felt if she could just love him enough, he would be healed. At times she judged him, other times herself. She entered a cycle of desperate attempts to make the relationship work, followed by his descent once again into pain and alcohol.

One day, after yet another failed rescue attempt, she was sitting quietly alone, exhausted and despairing, praying for guidance. As she struggled with what she should do next, she heard a voice. She had never heard a voice before, nor was she expecting an "answer" to her dilemma. Yet out of "nowhere" she heard a firm yet loving voice within her say, "You are in My way. He needs to come to Me on his knees for his healing. He is My son and I love him more than you could ever love him."

It is not for us to judge how others must find their inner peace. Though we often want to help those we love avoid pain, many will only come to their peace "on their knees." It is usually through our pain and challenges that our hearts are opened and the ego's grasp is weakened and finally released. Understandably, we often would like to intrude and rescue those we love from this painful process. Though we can always help by offering our unconditional love and compassion, we must also remember that their process is proceeding right on schedule for them, no matter how slow and painful it may appear to us.

In the last chapter I stressed the importance of reinterpreting our past. I know this sounds like I am saying just to decide to rewrite the past painful events in our personal histories so that they no longer rob your peace of mind. And I guess in a way that is what I am saying. However, this does not mean that an examination and understanding of our past, especially our childhood, is not helpful or should be avoided. There is an advantage to bringing our nightmares into our awareness, but only to learn that they, like all dreams, are not real.

By seeking a "clear picture" of our early "programming," we can more quickly and easily reprogram ourselves to be happy and peaceful. Many of us avoid examining our past because of the pain we fear we will reveal. We fear that if we raise our pain to our awareness, it may overwhelm us and drive us deeper into our depression, anger, and unhappiness. Indeed, without the proper "tools" this can happen. Mental institutions are full of people who have revealed their pain, but had no effective psychological or philosophical framework to eventually heal their wounds.

We may fear that honestly confronting our pain may give it greater reality. Therefore, we avoid looking at it. Will the pain just get worse? Is there any value to dredging it up? Can we really ever work through it? Will the rage be controllable? We need to realize that it is through confronting it that we are able to observe its illusion. Only by confronting our pain, acknowledging it, and allowing ourselves to experience it can we come to realize that it is self-made and that we, in the present, are responsible for it and that we can free ourselves from it.

Avoiding and denying our pain may seem to have some beneficial effects. By denial and avoidance we are able to delay the acutely painful period that is encountered when we finally decide to look at the full extent of our pain, our hatred, our rage, and our judgment. During this denial period our painful wounds may be subconsciously running, and often ruining, our lives. Even though this "dysfunctional comfort zone" has a constant level of dull pain, it may seem preferable to risking the intense pain that is possible if we decide to look at our deep-seated anger, pain, and fear. Instead of going through a shorter, more intense period of honestly confronting our pain, we allow it to slowly fester below the surface. As it remains unhealed and festering, our wounds rob our peace of mind, distort our relationships, and attack our bodies.

Sometimes a lifetime of this dull, constant pain is chosen rather than the more dynamic and intense experience of confronting the pain and finally healing it. Indeed, without the correct perception with which to reveal and understand our past wounds, delving into them too deeply can create even greater pain and despair. Without these "tools," it is often best to honor a person's desire to stay in denial. Forcing them out of it may create even greater fear.

However, a person may begin to alter their belief system. They may begin to seek to understand the inherent value and purpose in all the past events of their life, even the most painful. They are now developing a safe basis, a "safety raft" over the sea of pain, in which to begin to reveal their pain so that it may be healed.

As long as we believe in a random or punitive universe, there may be good reason to avoid facing the pain. If we perceive a random universe, we believe there is no beneficial purpose to our painful events. We just had bad luck. It should never have happened. If we fear a punitive universe, maybe our pain is the deserved punishment for our internal flaws or unloving actions, perhaps even those of another lifetime. These safety rafts are too full of holes to take us to the other side where we can find peace and forgiveness. Venturing out on our sea of pain in these faulty rafts can be disastrous. Without a worthy "safety raft" to take us across the pain to the peace on the other side, we may indeed sink and drown.

The only safety raft that will get us through to the other side is an understanding of the purpose of all the events in our lives, no matter how painful they may appear. We only need to change our mind about the purpose of the world. We need to change our perception to understand nothing "bad" has happened, or can ever happen, to us. At first this seems ludicrous or naïve, almost hardened. People have been abused, murdered, attacked, betrayed, ignored, humiliated, etc. How can these things not be "bad?"

However, we must also understand that we have chosen to interpret these events as painful and "bad" and, therefore, we feel justified in allowing them to continue to make us unhappy. Everything that has ever happened to us has offered us the optimal experience for our greatest growth, even if they seemed "bad." Once we understand this, we now have an adequate safety raft to venture forth. Though the voyage may at times be choppy, even threatening, as we continue to scramble on top of our raft each time we are thrown off, we will eventually reach the other side of peace and safety.

An example of how painful events can often be for our highest good is found in the life of Franklin Delano Roosevelt. The former president was stricken by polio at the height of his physical prowess. Most of us would agree that this was "bad" and it would have been much better for him if it had not happened. Yet listen to the interpretation of his wife, Eleanor:

> I would like to think that he would have done the things he did even without his paralysis, but knowing the streak of vanity and insincerity in him, I do not think he would have unless somebody had dealt him a blow between the eyes.
>
> (Doris Kearns Goodwin, *No Ordinary Time: Franklin and Eleanor Roosevelt: The Home Front in World War II,* New York: Touchstone Books, 1995)

But what of bad things that happen to us? They do not all seem necessary to teach a lesson. What about "bad" things that happen to innocent children? Often our greatest challenge (painful events) is also our greatest teacher. A childhood sickness can teach us compassion, patience, and how to live in the moment. An abusive childhood can teach us to overcome fear and develop greater self-reliance. A loss of a loved one in childhood can open our hearts and make us more understanding of others' pain. All these "bad things" can have tremendously beneficial results, if we change our perceptions regarding them. If we continue to perceive them as negative and bad, they can crush our spirits rather than enhance them.

If we are still wedded to the concept of blame, righteous indignation, justifiable anger, meaningless horrible events, revenge, etc., looking deeply at our pain can leave us with greater anger and despair. We can be set at sea, awash in anger at, or disbelief in, God for allowing "bad" things to happen. We will feel rage at our "enemies and oppressors" for doing "bad" things to us. We will wail against a random or punitive universe. The result of this "justifiable" anger is despair and depression. Only changing our belief system, our perceptions, so that we can reinterpret these past events, can save us from all this. We must begin to understand that all things work together for our good.

It is healing to recognize and feel our anger and pain, but it will not be, if we are continually attempting to justify it. Therefore, it is our intent in looking at our pain that will determine whether this searching will help us or harm us. If our real intent is to further justify our anger, our blame, our sense of being victimized, our unhappiness, then confronting our pain will only harm us. It will further solidify the illusion.

It is healing to recognize and feel our anger and pain, but it will not be, if we are continually attempting to justify it.

However, this justification may be a necessary step, for a period of time, towards our healing. Eventually we may decide that we no longer want the pain we have cherished and held so close. Now our intent in looking at our pain is to work towards love and forgiveness. Now we will pass to the other shore, where peace and comfort await. We must begin to examine our fear and pain, as only this breaking up of our emotional "logjam" will make room for feelings of love and safety.

Usually our pain has made us feel separate and alone, solitary in a lonely and even hostile universe. It is easily understandable how past "painful" events would make us feel this way. We need not judge or blame ourselves for having arrived at this conclusion. It is the core dilemma of our entire species. We interpret "attacks" (disguised calls for love) and painful events (growth lessons) as further proof of our unlovability or vulnerability, our separation from everyone, including God. It is this "pain of separation" that is at the core of all our pain. Unless we finally understand that we do not want this pain of separation, we will continue to accept it, even seek it, mistaking it for something we want.

The ego, our belief system in our separation, is threatened should we ever seek to find a "better way." Therefore, it continues to seek out this "hell" of justifiable anger under the guise of seeking the "heaven" of revenge and being right. It continues sternly on its path, offering us more and more self-created "proof" that we are all indeed alone and separate. "It was really unkind, even cruel, that I was treated like that. I deserve to be angry and in pain. Who would not be? My unhappiness today is caused by these painful past events." On and on our egos go with a constant stream of thoughts of separation and aloneness, blame and justifiable anger.

The Spiritual Bypass

As part of avoidance, denial, and minimizing, we may try a "spiritual bypass or spiritual Band-Aid." This involves applying a spiritual concept or belief as a Band-Aid over an emotional wound. We avoid looking at our pain and just pray more, or say more affirmations, or meditate more, or apply the appropriate spiritual cliché, or read more spiritual books, etc. We hope that God will magically remove our pain from us without us making any internal changes in our belief system or perceptions. However, since it is these perceptions and belief systems that are causing our pain, it is only by changing them that we can release our pain. No changes we make externally will make any difference, if we have not changed internally.

Often we offer others a quick spiritual bypass in our attempts to help them. They come to us with their pain and their despair and we quote them a spiritual or psychological cliché, rather than just being with them in their pain. We believe all we really have to do is to replace the painful feelings with the appropriate spiritual truth and the work is done. It is understandable how we would arrive at this conclusion. Many spiritual teachings seem to imply this would work. However, it does not. The inner work of searching out all our unhealed wounds, all our barriers to joining, must also be done.

It is when we have reached our full threshold of absorbing and experiencing this pain, that we may finally begin to conceive that there might be a different, less painful way of viewing our pain and our world. We have begun to understand the "hell" that is the pain of our feelings of separation. We have finally decided that we do not want this. Now our healing can begin.

Having decided that there must be a better way, we begin to observe all the conclusions that we reached, all the interpretations we have arrived at, in regards to our past. As we begin to look at our past, we may pass through this period of intense feelings described above. As we reveal our pain, our first inclination will be to blame ourselves or others. However, as we continue with this healing process, we will eventually see that our pain is not a given, it is no more real than we make it. We can choose otherwise. We can choose Heaven, not hell. It is only when the pain of our belief in separation is seen exactly as it is that we observe the "value" that we have placed on these thoughts. It is then that we realize it is this we do not want.

As we peel back the layers of our existing belief system, we will find that the underlying fear of looking at our pain is the fear that there will be no one there to deliver us from it. We do not trust that God will heal all wounds. We fear that we will be left alone in even greater pain and loneliness and we do not want to take that risk. So we avoid looking at our pain, forgetting that we are not alone. God will not leave us comfortless. All we need to do is our part by being willing to confront our pain, trusting that we will see its purpose and be delivered from it.

Assisting Others Through Their Pain

In 1975 I was living in Santa Cruz, California, a beautiful seaside town seventy miles south of San Francisco. Every Saturday morning I would drive to San Francisco to teach a class. I drove up through the congested Bay Area on Highway 101, but on my return trip Saturday afternoon I took the Pacific Coast Highway. This road runs along the ocean and is cut into the steep cliffs and meanders through mostly deserted countryside and has some of the most dramatically beautiful views in the country.

One Saturday, as I traveled home on that lonely stretch, I noticed two figures kneeling just in front of an old station wagon. Thinking something was wrong, and knowing how deserted the road was, I pulled over to offer assistance. As I approached, I realized that the figures were two young men, dressed as Buddhist monks, kneeling in prayer. I asked if they needed help. I thought maybe their car was broken and they were praying that it would be magically fixed. Neither stopped praying or acknowledged my presence. Looking around for an explanation, I noticed a sign in their car window. The sign explained that they were two young American Buddhist monks who were traveling up the West Coast and stopping to pray for world peace every few feet. Each night, one would return to their dilapidated station wagon and move it the few hundred yards they had progressed that day. The station wagon served as their bedroom and kitchen. Once a week they stopped at a store for food. They had also taken a vow of silence for this trip, which they expected to take a year or more.

I had no idea of it at the time, but for the next few months these two would become my "therapists," though they never said a word to me. What happened was this. Every Saturday, when I passed them (it took months for them to travel the seventy miles from Santa Cruz to San Francisco), I stopped to talk. In the beginning I would just rattle on about the week and my life in general. I would often kid them. "I bet I am the highlight of the week," I would say. "I know you guys are sincere, but I would bet all this praying and silence gets old at times. After all, you are an American like me. You were raised on *The Lone Ranger* and *Leave It to Beaver*. You probably partied at fraternity houses and danced at pop festivals. I bet some days you wonder, 'Is it Saturday yet? I hope it is so that guy can come by and babble for awhile. I could use a break from all this praying.' Or maybe not," I said. "Maybe you dread my visit and think, 'Oh, God! Here comes that idiot to break my peaceful meditation again. Who cares about his self-centered emotional dribble.' Anyway, I will never know since you guys are not talking."

After a few weeks of just general discussion and reflection (all on my part, of course), I began to discuss a problem I was having in my relationship with the woman I was seeing. It was one of those relationships that was heavy on the romantic, sexual aspects, but lacking elsewhere. Every week I began to explain what had occurred between us and how I was feeling about it. I would discuss my different alternatives from trying to love her "more purely" to leaving the relationship all together. Often I would complain of all the unloving ways she had treated me during the week, trying to arouse their agreement and sympathy. I was a "victim" and I wanted their compassion. All I got was their silence.

Sometimes I would try to get their response. I would set up different situations. "OK," I would say, "if you guys think this relationship is going nowhere and I should leave, just move your left arm a little. Just do that. That is not really breaking your vow of silence. And I would not act like you did anything, so your friend would not know you signaled. Come on, guys, you know all the background here, all the details, everything I have been thinking and feeling. Can you cut me a little slack?" But all I got was their silence.

After awhile I realized that what I needed was just someone to listen to me, someone who offered no opinions or judgments, no telling me of what they would do or what they thought I should do. Though I thought I wanted agreement as to how unjustly I was being treated, actually what I needed was someone to silently remind me I was choosing this perception. There was something healing and clarifying just talking to them about it. It was just someone to listen and I "sensed" they were doing so nonjudgmentally and, more importantly, with a sense that everything was fine and that I would find my own answers. It was almost as if in their silence they were saying, "You know your own answers. Just keep talking and listening to yourself. In time you will know what to do." Maybe I was just projecting this onto them. After all, they were Buddhist and Buddhists were supposed to believe that all life is an illusion. Maybe just me thinking that they were thinking it was all okay was enough.

As the weeks passed, I did sort things out and finally decided to leave the relationship. Just listening once a week to my fears and rationalizations stated out loud made many things clear to me. At my last visit (the next week they would have prayed past my entry point to Highway 1), I thanked them for all they had "done," or rather not done, and told them I had left a box of food in their car as a gift. I confessed the box contained some treats and a *MAD* magazine, just in case they were interested. I told them I knew they would miss me and that I thought that I had probably been the highlight of this portion of their journey, as I was probably the only one who really shared my heart with them.

As I got up to leave, one of them lifted his head and turned towards me and winked. It was the first time either of them had looked at me in all those months. And there was something in his face that made me think that I had not been the only person who had been baring his soul to them, that there had been others, maybe many others. In their silence, these "therapists" were indeed helping to make the world more peaceful. Though I had no way of knowing it in the beginning, I was sent the exact "therapists" I needed.

"Therapists" are not only those people who have been professionally trained as such. Nor are "patients" only those who seek out professional therapy. Rather we are all at times therapists and at other times patients. Therefore, every human interaction has the potential for therapy and healing. The instant we are ready to release a fear, the proper "therapist" will be brought to us. It may be a "professional therapist" or a compassionate friend. It may be just something we overhear in a conversation or read in a book. It does not matter. As soon as we are ready to recognize and release our fears, we will create the needed mechanism.

True Empathy

Whenever we are talking with our mates or friends about their pain and problems, we feel the desire to help them and to in some way alleviate their pain. In addition to our advice, we may offer them our "empathy" in our attempts to help. Empathy is described as "the action of understanding, being aware of, being sensitive to, and vicariously experiencing the feelings, thoughts, and experience of another of either the past or present...." We think that by really feeling their pain and their hurt with them, that this will be helpful to them. In reality, the opposite is true. This type of empathy only helps to make their pain "real."

If a friend comes to us and tells us what an awful thing has happened to them or how unjustly someone has treated them, our immediate inclination is to offer them agreement that indeed something bad has happened. When we do this, the person may seem to experience temporary relief, as usually it is just this attitude and response that they are seeking. However, when we offer this response we are not offering them any real assistance in permanently releasing them from their pain. We are rather solidifying their pain by agreeing that it is a necessary reaction inherent in their predicament.

They believe they are sitting on a bench in hell and if someone will just come sit on the bench with them, they will no longer be in hell or at least they will not be alone there. They will attempt to ask anyone who will listen to join them on that bench and commiserate together about how horrible it is. But the reality is, even if we sit on that bench with them, they still believe they are in hell. We can serve them best by reminding them, often silently, that their "bench in hell" is only an illusion. This means we allow them to experience their pain. This is something we all need to do. We do not need to invalidate it. However, we do not need to agree that their pain is something negatively inherent in the situation. We can agree with them that their feelings are understandable and valid, without agreeing that they are necessary.

"True empathy" does not mean to join in another's suffering, no matter how much they would like us to. When we do this, we form another "special relationship" based on the shared suffering. When we do this our ego is joining with another ego mistakenly believing that we can lessen the pain by entering into it and sharing it. In reality, we only increase the pain when we do this. "True empathy" means recognizing that we (our egos) never know what will bring another healing and peace. We can never know what needed qualities and awareness a person's "painful" predicaments can create. Only Spirit knows this.

To really empathize means to not make the past and the pain real. Usually, however, we do the opposite. When we agree with someone that something terrible has occurred, we do not encourage them to look for the growth and spiritual value inherent in every situation. We solidify the belief that "nightmares" can occur and that we are never truly safe. We agree with their perception that some things are "good" and others "bad." We agree that the anger, pain, and blame are justifiable. We reinforce their fears instead of helping to guide them through to the truth. Where we had sought to release them, we are instead imprisoning them. We can serve them best by reminding ourselves that we no longer need to believe in nightmares of any kind.

If we offer "true empathy," it must come from a sense of humility by understanding that we never know what will bring peace to another. Just because they are choosing to view a situation painfully does not indicate that the situation does not have the ability to bring them peace. Though we do not know what will bring peace, God does. If we will do our part by letting go of our judgment of the situation and not join the suffering, God will offer "true empathy" through us.

This often involves communication on a nonverbal level. We can compassionately listen to their predicament while holding an image of them growing through their pain. If a person is not yet ready to look at the blessing in their pain, it will only anger them if we point it out to them. Indeed, they may need to seek out someone else who is willing to sit on that bench in hell with them. They may still feel if another person will understand and feel their pain, then it will greatly lessen. It will not. Only a change in their perception will do that.

Chapter 7

Letting Go of Fear

et me share with you another chapter in my personal odyssey of releasing my fears and creating a peaceful relationship. A year after my wife, Julia, and I met and the honeymoon period was winding down, we both confronted our wall of fear. For each of us the wall was quite different in appearance, but in reality it was the same wall, fear. Julia's appeared as a wall of fear of commitment. Julia and her family had moved many times in eighteen years before she left her parents' home. At a very young age she quickly learned the pain of making a loving friend only to have the friendship permanently ripped away with her parents' next move. By the time we met, she was struggling to let go of her belief system that all relationships last a short while and then you move on to the next one. This belief had sabotaged several of her earlier romantic relationships.

Though my childhood had been more stable than Julia's, my parents, though loving, had often been inattentive. This left me with a belief that, though I was loved, I was not very important or special. My belief system, as I described earlier, was that I would find a wonderful mate and she would leave me for a "better man," that I would not be "in their league." I feared I just did not matter. I just was not that important to people.

By the time we met, we had both been working hard to release these fears. The intense energy of our initial contact and the Stage 1 "honeymoon" period that followed, fooled us into believing that we had completely released them. But months after we met they reared their ugly heads for one last attempt to assert themselves and destroy yet another relationship. Stage 2 was becoming intense.

Julia, fearing we were getting too close and pain was just around the corner, began to distance herself from our relationship. She began to see another man, and yes, he was taller, more handsome, and had more hair than I did (damned by my genetic deficiencies again!). I was creating my worst long-awaited fears. I was creating another "better man." Both of us were living out our fears again. Both of us fell back into our fear-based responses (our well worn path).

As she had done before in other relationships, she told me she did not want a long-term committed relationship in her life. It was time to change partners (i.e., the family was moving again). As I had done in past relationships, I retreated bravely, trying to keep some vestige of pride and dignity (a better man had won my lady). We broke up.

During our time apart, we both began to seriously look at the fears that had destroyed yet another relationship. Also, we missed each other. Our connection had been very deep. One night I sat with a friend discussing our breakup. Through my discussions with my friend I began to see clearly this fear I had had since adolescence. I actually saw it as a visual image. "My woman" and another man riding off into the sunset on his gallant steed, me waving forlornly goodbye, looking frumpy and sad. Meaning me no intentional harm, they would even turn and smile, testifying to their greater spiritual and emotional advancement. What an image! It was the pictorial representation of my belief system of unworthiness that had sat in the back of my head for twenty years, creating painful relationship after painful relationship. I had never consciously noticed it before.

As I drove from my friend's house, I began to laugh. What a ridiculous image! How had I let it ruin so many relationships without even knowing it? I decided then and there it would sabotage no more. I turned the car towards Julia's house and began the hour drive from Berkeley to Palo Alto.

On the way down, I felt elated. I realized that I was on the top of my wall of fear and about to jump over. I had no idea what I would find when I arrived. Maybe my worst fear—Julia in a passionate embrace with the "better man," with both of them looking annoyed at the interruption. However, now it did not matter to me. I knew that just by going down there and being willing to confront that fear, that I had ventured in to a new land that I had always been afraid to go to before. I would no longer walk my well-worn path of a quiet but dignified retreat from a relationship that I mistakenly believed that I did not deserve.

When I arrived, Julia was alone (having let go of the fear of seeing her with another man I guess I no longer needed to create it). For an hour I told her everything I had realized in one of the clearest communications in my life. I told her of my pitiful self-image and that now I had realized that I was the knight in shining armor (even if I looked less the part). I understand that even though I was a long way from being "perfect" and always loving, I was usually caring and kind and willing to give as well as receive, and therefore, now knowing and believing this, I was ready for a successful relationship.

I told her that if she did not think I was her knight, it did not matter, because the next relationship I created would be free of the fears that had ruined all the rest. I would be the prince charming in the next relationship and she could choose whether it would be with her or not. At that moment it really did not matter to me. I was ecstatic to finally have understood and released my fear. I was free of the fear and knew that I was also free of the painful relationships it had created. I left her house feeling as free and complete as I ever had and with a wonderful sense of anticipation as to what the future would bring. I knew that long-held fear would never warp and destroy another relationship. Within weeks, Julia released much of her fear and we have been together ever since.

These and other fears do still creep into our relationship, however, they no longer have the power to destroy it. Their power is reduced to keeping us in a separated, painful place for a few hours (occasionally a day) until we once again identify the fear and let it go. Though we did not then, nor have we yet, completely released these fears, we have reduced them so that they no longer dominate the relationship. They affect us, but no longer rule us.

Placating Our Fears: Denial in Motion

We need to understand that these fears have been part of us for a long time, perhaps most of our lives. Julia and I had been building our belief systems since childhood, through adolescence and through previous relationships. Situations and relationships will trigger these fears at various times. Though these situations are often perceived as curses, punishments, or just bad luck, they are rather blessings or opportunities for us to recognize and release our fears. We need to always ask, "What is the lesson for me here?" Unless we are asking this of every relationship and situation in our lives, we will miss its purpose. We will either think it is random and meaningless and, therefore, has no purpose, or we will blame it on things and people outside ourselves and assign it a purpose other than its true one, as a lesson for us to learn to love.

Often, just when we are finally ready to understand a certain fear and let it go, we will precipitate a major incident that triggers our fears to their maximum intensity. Julia and I did this a year after we met. This situation may appear very frightening. If we fear rejection, as I did, we may precipitate a situation where real or perceived rejection is a possible, perhaps probable, outcome. If we fear commitment, as Julia did, we may have to decide to commit to a relationship or lose it. If we fear that we can never give enough, we may have to do or say something that will be perceived by another as not giving them what they are "demanding" from us. If we fear confrontation, we may precipitate an event where confrontation is unavoidable.

Usually we have created similar situations in the past, since they are being formed by our still intact fear-based belief system. Usually we have followed a fearful response. In the past we have avoided the confrontation and chosen a response determined and dictated by our fears. The thought of reacting entirely differently than our usual fear-based responses may appear so frightening that it is almost unimaginable to us. Could we really tell our mate that we no longer can tolerate unconscious, unloving behavior? Could we really encourage our mate's spiritual and emotional growth, and trust that if they no longer neurotically needed us, they would still maturely want us? Could we really decide to love ourselves and cease creating the painful relationships born in self-condemnation?

It is much easier to placate our fears rather than to release them. Eventually, they will emerge again. Julia and I would have been only placating our fears had we stayed apart. Placating our fears just involves removing the perceived threat so that it is no longer an immediate danger. The fear is not gone; it has only temporarily receded. The emphasis here is on "temporarily." We do this by avoiding potentially painful situations or denying them should they occur. Often we simply react to them with our patterned fear-based responses and they are "resolved" only to occur again in a similar form.

For instance, if our mate is feeling threatened by our spiritual and emotional growth, we may fearfully choose to avoid discussing this with them. Perhaps we are afraid of their anger or estrangement. Perhaps we are afraid they will ridicule our initial efforts towards change. We may fear it will adversely effect their fragile low self-esteem (that may be preventing them from pursuing a similar search). We may fear that their reaction to our growth will be such that separation or divorce may occur. We may fear risking and perhaps losing the relationship. We fearfully continue avoiding this area with them. We rationalize that we do this to keep harmony in the family and not increase our mate's fears. We have placated the fear by avoiding it, but it is still there with the same influence over both people.

Rather than placate it through avoidance and denial, we can decide to release our fear. We can understand that there is nothing to fear. If they are angry, they need to go through that and it is not proof of our unworthiness, because someone is upset with us. If it adversely effects their feelings about themselves, then this will give them another opportunity to examine the faulty basis of their low self-esteem. If it threatens to end the relationship, then it just means that they need to remain in a fear-based relationship and are not yet ready to awaken. A clearer more loving relationship is still perceived as a threat to them.

We can approach them directly but nonjudgmentally with our growth knowing that nothing "bad" can result from this. By making a decision for our own self-growth, the results will not injure anyone even if it causes someone anger, which at a surface level appears as injury. Indeed the other person's reaction may be anger or withdrawal. Since we are no longer being run by this fear, we can celebrate our releasing of a fear that has long held sway over us and our relationship. We can anticipate the peace and joy this newfound freedom will bring into our life, even though we are not sure what new "form" our relationship will take. We are on the other side of our fear and all our present and future relationships will reflect this new freedom.

Often, when we are ready to release a long-held fear that has been affecting a relationship, this may cause a variety of reactions within the other person. They may become angry, depressed, withdrawn, violent, sullen, or fearful. Their own fears may have been dovetailing with our fears in this relationship and they may not yet have decided to work on releasing theirs. We may perceive their intense negative reactions to our growth as yet one more barrier to our releasing our fears. Actually, their reactions, no matter how unpleasant it may seem, is a blessing to more clearly expose our fear and mirror it back to us. Our fear of them becoming depressed, angry, withdrawn, etc., is part of our work. We need to release our fears concerning their reaction to our letting go of our fears. Whatever emotions they experience are part of their growth to release their fears and we are not responsible for these emotions, even if they are "sure" we are.

They may still choose to "sleep" longer and attempts to awaken them will only create anger. Having understood our own fearful belief system we can have greater compassion towards them. Having awakened sooner, we can gently help them by offering unconditional love.

Whatever our great fears are with regard to our mated relationships, we know our own all too well. They are the ones that cause the huge knot in our stomach when we even think about confronting them. They are the ones that, when we contemplate a course of action that is different from our usual fearful response, make us tell ourselves, "Oh no, I could never do that. That would be terrible." We must remember that in these circumstances, fear and its creator, the ego, are making a tremendous effort to convince us that the fears are valid and should be listened to and obeyed. Whatever the fears, until they are confronted and released, they will cause us to continually create these painful situations. The pain is our alarm that a fear is present that needs to be resolved so that the alarm can be turned off. The alarm will stay on until it is no longer needed.

This concept is not the same as "conquering" your fears. When we decided to fight our fears in hope of conquering them, we are making illusions real. If we believe the fear is real, we still believe it exists and threatens us, but that we, at least for now, have been able to "overpower it." Rather, to release a fear is to understand that it was never "real" or appropriate to the situation. It is the asking of what love would say in this situation instead of what fear says. It is simple to replace the fear-based perception of the ego with the perception of love. It was only an illusion that something "bad" might happen or some punishment was impending. There was never any reason to fear nor was there any real fear to be conquered.

A Safe World

It is very frightening to feel that perhaps we may never free ourselves from our fears. Many of us have this fear, though it is seldom discussed. Most self-help books, therapies, and spiritual paths are involved with confronting and releasing our fears, however, they seldom address our very basic fear that we may never be able to adequately do this. To begin to truly release our fears we must begin to shift our perception from one of a hostile world, full of threats and dangers, to a perception of a safe world where nothing "bad" can ever happen to us.

The immediate response that arises to this concept is that awful, terrible things do happen to people every day. Accidents, sickness, wars, failures, betrayals, all occur with alarming frequency. If these things are occurring, how can it be true that nothing "bad" can ever happen to us? How can we ever feel truly safe in this world? How can we never not know fear?

It is not asked that we deny that these things are happening, only that we change our perceptions of these events. All events and circumstances work together for our highest good. There are no exceptions to this except from the ego's perspective. Everything "bad" or painful that happens to us can be perceived differently. Everything in our life is a gift to help us grow and learn. We never know what form this gift will take. Sometimes it will be a "happy" form (birth of a child, financial success, a happy marriage, etc.). Sometimes it may be a painful form (death, sickness, divorce, "failure"). They are all simply forms of a gift. Sometimes we need pain to grow and change, other times not. We never know what will bring us peace.

All events and circumstances work together for our highest good.

For instance, if the body's function is as a communication vehicle, not a pleasuring tool, this function can be served as easily with a "damaged" body as a "healthy" one. If love is eternal and we are always united with our loved ones, even after death, then death is not "bad." If death is merely a peaceful transition to another stage of consciousness as is reported by almost all people who have had "near death experiences," then death can be reconciled and understood as not invalidating the concept of a safe world.

No matter what painful events have occurred in our lives, joy and happiness are always available to us through God's love and grace. We never know what events and situations are most needed for us to learn. What in the past has been perceived as a catastrophe can be reinterpreted as an event that will bring new people and lessons into our life to assist our growth.

The High Wall of Fear

In addition to perceiving the illusion and inappropriateness of our fears, there is another effective method of getting past these deeply ingrained fears. This is to begin to understand, desire, and anticipate the joy and freedom that will be available to us once we have released our fears and they no longer enslave us. It is as if for our entire lives we have gone along the same well-worn path until we arrive at a large, high wall (our fears) that blocks our progress. We have always stopped on this side of the wall and do not even know what is on the other side. The wall appears so impenetrable and so high that anything other than stopping and turning around (fear-based responses) seems unimaginable to us. We believe we could do almost anything but scale that wall.

The wall may appear in many forms in our love life. Perhaps we fear commitment (the wall) so we are always leaving relationships when they require commitment (the well-worn path). Scaling the wall is resolving our fears about commitment. Perhaps we fear that we are not lovable (the wall) so we are always creating relationships in which we do not feel loved (the well-worn path). Scaling this wall would be to realize that we are all lovable and then transforming our existing relationship or creating a new one. Maybe the wall is feeling we have little worth except as an object of sexual pleasure and romantic fantasy. The worn path is a series of relationships that do not endure the "honeymoon" period. Our freedom here is in realizing that who we each are is much greater than a physical body and that physical pleasuring and being "in love" is only an illusion of a truly loving relationship.

Once we have decided that there must be another way, the change begins. When we begin to perceive our fears as unneeded, unwanted, and inappropriate, we have begun to scale the wall. Rather than retreat from the wall as usual, we can begin to try various methods to scale the wall. Initially these may be awkward endeavors or angry flailing at ourselves, the wall itself, or others whom we perceive as having built the wall. Eventually as we accept that it was we, not others, who carefully built and adamantly protected our wall, the anger subsides. To scale the wall we must stop blaming either ourselves or others and understand that we, and they, just mistakenly chose fear and that we can decide differently. In time, we may decide to scale the wall in one or several great leaps. Or we may decide to slowly dismantle the wall, brick by brick. It is our choice. After all, it is our wall.

Once we have resolved these fears, they no longer dictate our behavior. They may reappear but with a greatly diminished hold on us, and they will no longer dictate our action, though they may influence it. Fear may be one of many emotions we feel, but it will no longer be the dominant one. It may continue to cause some anxiety and worry, but we will be able to reestablish our peace and clarity as we once again recognize our fears and place them within our new perspective. A major change will have taken place in this area of our life, as trust, love, and self-esteem replace fear and self-condemnation as our dominant emotions. Fulfillment, peace, and joy will replace conflict, pain, and confusion.

We are on the other side of the wall. The wall is behind us and no longer impedes our progress and growth. We have never been on this side of the wall. On this side are new adventures, new insights, new feelings. On this side we are free of our fears and the painful relationships they created. On this side is a greater peace and happiness. Whatever relationships we create now will be free of these crippling fears.

We do not have to be free of all of our fear to scale the wall. We just need to reduce it until it is no longer the dominant emotion. Its previous position as dominant is now replaced by our faith that we can have loving relationships and our belief in our own value and worth. Soon a situation will arise that, in the past, we would have responded to in our usual fearful manner. Now we will have the opportunity to respond from our courage and faith. We will have scaled the wall. We can even arrive at the point at which, rather than dreading these situations that before we had allowed our fears to dominate, we can actually anticipate them as they will provide us another opportunity to free ourselves from our fears.

Anticipating the Watershed Event

An example of anticipating a defining moment of fear, rather than dreading it, occurred in another area of my life, my relationship with my daughter, Julie. My wife, Julia (yes, the names are confusing to me, too), was usually the heavyweight in discipline and more willing to allow Julie to suffer the consequences of her actions. I was more likely to come to her rescue and bail her out. Several years ago, when she was in college, we bought her a car with agreements on things she must do to keep it (good grades, change oil, not lend it to friends, use the charge card for emergencies only, etc.). Like most teenagers, she broke most of the agreements. After several warnings, and several blatant broken agreements, my wife felt it was time to take the car away.

Once again, I tried to rescue Julie, though I too felt the car should go. As I looked at my conflicting feelings, I realized that certain major fears were in play here. Generally, I feared that if I did not give people what they wanted from me, they would not love me or it may indicate selfishness or unfairness on my part. Specifically, I feared if we took Julie's car away, she would be angry with us and withdraw her love (though she has never done this). I also feared we might be negatively affecting her enjoyable life as a college student.

Once I understood these fears, I realized that they, rather than my clarity and good judgment, were dictating my decisions. I realized that if I needed to give someone everything they wanted from me to keep their love, something was wrong with the relationship and needed to be corrected. I became willing, actually eager, to tell her we were taking her car and incur her wrath. I no longer needed to fear that I would lose her love or be unfair. I told Julia to let me be the one to tell Julie we were taking her car away, something I had dreaded doing before and was going to ask Julia to do.

When Julie called, I told her of our decision and yes, there were the tears and pleading and anger we had expected. When she arrived home several hours later to drop the car off, I was in the yard. "I guess you are pretty mad at me," I said as she got out of the car. "No, I am mad at myself," was her response. I was amazed. Having made peace with my decision, she knew blaming would not work and this allowed her to look at the true cause of her pain. She was taking responsibility for her actions! We both hugged and laughed. We drove her back to school without a trace of tension during the trip. The car was soon sold.

That was a defining moment in my fear in raising my daughters. Our continued insistence that they be responsible for their actions and our refusal to take their pain away has helped them grow into mature and responsible young women. Our willingness to always love them, but not to always rescue them, has created a closeness between the four of us that we all cherish.

By keeping in mind the invalid and faulty basis of our fears, as well as the uplifting benefits, we will finally be letting them go. We can actually reach a state where we are eagerly anticipating, instead of dreading, the circumstances that will allow us to confront these fears. By changing our perceptions concerning an event, we can now anticipate this event as a truly transformational moment in our growth and development. We can look forward to being free of these fears and experiencing the peace and clarity this freedom will bring. Just knowing that we are finally confronting this ancient fear can bring us joy. Instead of dreading the situation, we can welcome it, knowing we are about to do something that in the past we have been too fearful to do. We are ending a pattern, letting go of a long-held fear.

When the time comes to finally confront a situation and take the action or make the statement that is based on our clarity and courage instead of our fears, we may feel anxious and nervous, as we are confronting a major change in our life. We are scaling the wall. However, mixed with this anxiety is a sense of excitement we may remember feeling as children when it was the first day of school or camp or as teenagers when we left home or went to college. It was both scary and exciting. But above all it was something that we knew we had to do and very much wanted to do.

We do not need to rush this transformational event. When we are ready to encounter it, it will present itself. If our fears temporarily take control and cause us to retreat once again down our well-worn path, we do not need to worry or judge ourselves for lacking courage. We will be given an infinite number of opportunities to free ourselves from our fears. And we will be freed the moment we are willing to free ourselves. Sometimes this freeing is a very slow progressive process. We need to be gentle with ourselves and know that if we continue with our inner search and healing, our fears will finally subside to the point where we will be able to release them.

The Fear of Fear

I attended a workshop recently where I was asked to close my eyes and approach a door, knock, and ask to meet my "sub-personality," any fearful part of me (my ego). My self-critic answered the door. This is the part of me that always thinks I do not do enough, that I am not enough. He affects my days by telling me I should always be doing something different, something better. He influences my decisions as I seek to placate his insatiable appetite to accomplish and lead a "perfect" life. He undermines my joy as he removes me from the present by criticizing my past and warning me of my future.

As I confronted him at this door, I realized I hated this guy. But more importantly, I realized I feared he was more powerful than I. After all, for over twenty years I have actively tried to remove him from his home in my brain and he is still there! I could almost feel him taunting me, "Think you can get rid of me, do you? Forget it! I am more powerful than you and I will never leave. I will always run your life. Nanananaa!"

The next step of the exercise was to go with him to a beautiful field. The workshop leader put on soothing music and told us to be with our "sub-personality," our egos. As the music played, I began to play with him as if he were a child—a petulant, rebellious, headstrong child, but a child nonetheless. As we played, I realized I was stronger than he was, but like an insecure parent, I had given him the power. I stopped hating him and began to love him, to feel his confusion, his fear. I gently took the power back, as you would from a child once you realize there really is no struggle, that you have control. As I did that, I felt him relax and soften. It was as if he was saying, "Thank God you did that. I really needed someone to just stop me. I never really wanted my way. We have both been miserable in here. Let us just play together."

We really do have the power over our inner child, but we tremendously fear that we cannot control them and stop them from draining our lives. We do not need to fight with this child over control. This just continues the power struggle and the illusion that there is any real question as to who has ultimate control. Our ego is this inner child and, like all parents, we can decide to take the control back when we are ready. It was we who gave it away.

Chapter 8

Forgiveness: The Key to the Door to Heaven

*F*or several days I have been searching for the right story to lead into this chapter. I had finally chosen one, but it did not feel quite right. Yesterday a friend came over to visit Julia and me and she told us her story, and I knew it was the one to introduce this chapter. It is a wonderful story of true forgiveness.

Our friend had been sexually abused as a child by six different people in her family in her grandparents' generation, all of whom died many years ago. Though she had consciously suppressed the memories of the abuse, for many years this had caused her much pain and anguish. She started to tell us of her healing, which she had been actively pursuing for many years. She had approached her healing both psychologically and spiritually.

"Not long ago I realized my healing was finally complete," she said. "I began drawing a picture to release some fears I was having that my cancer might have returned. I noticed I was drawing six figures and I knew immediately who they were. I was surprised that I was no longer drawing them as horror figures, as I had done before, but rather as angels. I noticed that their colors were soft and they were translucent.

"I felt their presence in the room. I picked up a crayon and began to write what they were saying to me. They told me how sorry they were for what had happened, that they were whole and healed now and how much they loved me. They asked how they could help me now.

"I replied, 'I welcome you six angels. You are welcome here. We are free to love each other now. I am at peace with it now. I rest in peace.'

"Sometime after this event," Diane continued, "I felt that I had graduated from 'incest school' and I actually felt love and gratitude for having had the opportunity to attend. I knew then that my healing was complete. The picture is an ongoing reminder that this is so."

Our Mates Are Our Saviors or Our Crucifiers

Our mates are saviors or crucifers? Now there is an interesting thought. Again it is one of those thoughts that seems borderline absurd when you first hear it. But consider it in this context. It is through our relationships that we can be "saved or crucified." By this I mean we can choose to crucify ourselves with the pain of our judgments or to save ourselves from pain through our forgiveness. We can choose either Heaven or hell, "at-one-ment or at-lone-ment." The choice is up to us. It is through our relationships that we can perpetuate the illusion of our "alone-ment." This is true for every relationship that we are involved in, no matter how incidental or unimportant it may appear. However, in the mated relationship this is often more easily recognized and understood.

If we continue to misunderstand who our mates (and others) are and see them as flawed and/or sinful individuals, deserving of our judgment, condemnation, correction, and perhaps punishment, we have chosen to make them our crucifiers. We will be nailing ourselves to the cross of our own judgments. Even those people whom we perceive as our opponents or enemies are in reality part of our peace. When we attack them, verbally or physically, we give up this peace.

By condemning them, we have condemned ourselves. By forgetting who they are, we have forgotten who we are. And this is hell. If you believe differently, stop a moment and observe the personal hells we have all chosen for ourselves. The wars, the betrayals, the anger, the violence, the hate, the condemnation, all forms of hell we have banished ourselves to by our judgments of ourselves and each other.

We can choose otherwise. We can choose our mates, ourselves, and everyone else we come into contact with to be our savior instead of our crucifier. What is meant by the term savior? Our savior is someone who rescues or delivers us. What we need rescuing from is our judgments, our "original sin of forgetting" (not our original "sin"). Others can offer us this deliverance because it is through our interaction with them that we can observe our constant judging. By observing this, and understanding that it is inaccurate, unneeded, and unproductive, we can begin to release it. By releasing our judgment of others, we can begin to see them as they really are. Our eyes will be opened not to be right or wrong, good or bad, but rather we will see their beauty and their holiness, regardless of the appearance their fears have caused them to take.

They have then become our saviors, saving us from the hell of our own judgments. Diane's six "enemies," when perceived through the eyes of love, were really her saviors. At some deep level, she understood that. However, we can all see the inherent problems in referring to someone's childhood abusers as their saviors. In the world's terms this is unacceptable, naïve at best, callous and insensitive at worst.

We are all, at various times, in conflict with our mates. The people we are in the greatest conflict with are our best teachers of love. They are uncovering for us all the ways that we are unwilling to offer love. They may appear to be our greatest crucifiers, nailing us to the agony of our cross with their perceived attacks, flaws, or sins. In reality they offer the potential to be our greatest saviors, reminding us of their, and our, holiness. They are pushing our limits of loving, asking us to see their inner beauty in spite of their discordant outer form. Is not this what we are asking others to do for us? Is not this simply another application of the Golden Rule to "love another as you would love yourself"? We can be grateful to everyone who comes into our lives. Some come extending love, others come calling for our love with what appears to be "attacks." All offer us the opportunity to perceive love.

The Illusion of Forgiveness: Forgiving-to-Destroy

True forgiveness is the one essential ingredient in the formation of a healed relationship. Judgment, condemnation, and punishment soon become major forces in marriages, especially after we have left the Stage 1 "honeymoon" period, during which both partners are perceived as "almost perfect." During this "honeymoon period" we feel, "I would not want to change a thing about them." As this period recedes, and it always does, we begin to feel we would like to change many things. In truth it is these judgements that make us feel separate from each other, which is the goal of the ego. We often reach the insane state of believing that we cannot really feel happy until the other has changed. We then start to blame our unhappiness on them. We have entered Stage 2, the special hate relationship.

In addition to these overall judgments of some of their flaws and faults, we have catalogued specific incidents, in which we believe they have wronged us. These include all the slights, injustices, betrayals, inconsiderations, lapses in loving behavior, and "attacks" of all kinds. Some we have chosen to "forgive," others we have not. None have we forgotten and all we have made "real." These build up over the life of the marriage. They become part of the marriage's history and its highly valued scorecard. The power shifts between the partners as the score shifts in favor of one then the other. These unhealed incidents, and their ensuing emotions, form a hard shell around the relationship and do not allow its inner beauty to shine through. True forgiveness can dissolve this shell.

It is through forgiveness we find inner peace and bring true healing into our relationships. However, it is important to understand that it is not the traditional meaning of the word "forgiveness" that is intended here. The dictionary defines forgiving as "to give up resentment against or the desire to punish; stop being angry with." These concepts would be included in the true definition of forgiveness. However, the reasons we would not seek punishment or are not angry with someone are different from those usually associated with forgiveness.

Usually we forgive because we have decided that even though the person has unjustly attacked or injured us, we will, in our magnanimity, not seek retribution. We may not seek retribution for a variety of reasons, from motives ranging from pity to disguised attack. But the key here is we still believe in the "reality" of the attack and that we have indeed been unjustly treated and they deserve retribution, should we decide to seek it. However, we may decide to "forgive" and pardon. This is "forgiving-to-destroy," whereby we make their attack real and then decide to overlook it.

This only confirms that they have indeed "sinned" against us and should feel "guilty." Also we add to their guilt by contrasting their "badness" with our "goodness," exemplified by our ability to forgive their "evil" towards us. We, being the better of the two, will forgive. Now they feel not only flawed, but inferior to their magnanimous "victim." In this way we make the attack real and, therefore, we make the person's "sin" against us real. This adds to their sense of guilt and this concept of "forgiveness" may even greatly heighten it. In this way it is no forgiveness at all.

Our reason and our ego confirm that indeed their attack was real. The consequences of the attack are there for us to see as "proof" of their unjust treatment toward us. We look at an injured body, a betrayed relationship, a stolen object, the pain of an unloving word or deed, and see this as "evidence" of the reality of the attack. How can we possibly say that their "sin" against us is not real when the proof lies before us? These we perceive as proof of their sin. They deserve counterattack and retribution. The justified counterattack can be avoided only by the charitableness of our decision to forgive.

Attack and the withholding of forgiveness always involves anger. Anger involves the projection of separation and blame onto another. We do this to avoid taking responsibility for our own perceptions and reactions to others and their actions.

Anger comes from three beliefs:

1) that we have been attacked,
2) that our counterattack is, therefore, justified, and
3) we are, therefore, not responsible for our counterattack.

These three beliefs are essential for anger to occur. We then decide that the other is worthy of our attack on them. All these faulty conclusions must be recognized and released for true forgiveness to occur. After all, we were not told to "judge but then forgive" but rather to "judge not."

We mistakenly interpret God's forgiveness in the same way. We feel we have sinned and deserve to be punished. We feel that if we can only appeal to God's grace, then perhaps we can be spared painful punishment. We appeal to Him through all types of magic (lighting candles, prayers of supplication and intercession, confessionals, bargaining, purchasing icons, etc.), all in the hope of triggering God's pardon. And in our hearts we fear none of it will work. We have made God in our image and forgotten it was we who were made in His image (unconditional love). Since we are condemning and judgmental, we assume He must be. God does not want to punish us for our faults and "sins" but to heal us. We do not have to seek God's forgiveness because He has never condemned us. Only fear condemns and Love (God) always forgives and undoes what the fear has produced. Being made in Love's image we can strive to do likewise.

True Forgiveness

There is another view of forgiveness, one in which our ego, which is wedded to the idea of attack and retaliation, will strongly resist. Real forgiveness rests in realizing that we were never wronged, that the other person has not done anything to us. It maintains that the attack never really existed in the first place. At first glance this seems almost ludicrous, but follow the logic.

———————

Real forgiveness rests in realizing that we were never wronged,
that the other person has not done anything to us.

———————

Perceiving another's "attacks" and "flaws" as real and worthy of our anger and judgement indicates that we have misperceived them. Only loving thoughts are true. Everything else is an appeal for healing and help, regardless of the form it takes. We have viewed their behavior through our egos, not our love. In doing so, we have misunderstood where the correction may be found. It is never found by our pointing to the flaw and making it real, but rather by offering them the love and healing they are asking for. As we offer this to another, we are offering it to ourselves.

Another reason that an attack is not real is that what we thought was done to us, we actually did to ourselves. This is true because only we can deprive ourselves of our peace of mind (God's peace). It is not their action that upsets our peace. Rather, it is our response to, and perception of, this "attack" that robs us of our peace. If someone attacks or "harms" us, we can choose our reaction. We can choose forgiveness and peace or we can choose pain and judgment.

This concept that we can choose our experience by determining how we will react internally to external events can be demonstrated in its clearest form by a comment by author Viktor Frankl. Frankl survived the German concentration camps and observed a part of human nature that many missed. In *Man's Search for Meaning* (New York: Washington Square Press, 1998), he noted:

> We who lived in concentration camps can remember the men who walked through the huts comforting others, giving away their last piece of bread. They may have been few in number, but they offered sufficient proof that everything can be taken away from a man, but one thing: the last of the human freedom to (determine one's) attitude in any given set of circumstances, to choose one's own way.

In contrast to the ego's forgiveness that reinforces the other has sinned, true forgiveness reminds the other person that they have never sinned, that they can never sin. Forgiveness reminds the other of their eternal perfection, instilled in them by their Creator. True forgiveness means understanding that the attack was an illusion and was not real, that it never occurred, and that the other person is in no way flawed. True forgiveness reminds the other of their true identity as a flawless and sinless Child of God. It is also the ability to see that person in the holy present, not in the light of their past actions.

Forgiveness is a wake-up call to the other who has temporarily fallen asleep. We must gently awaken them, not condemn them to deeper sleep. If we were to awaken a young child from a bad dream, we would do so with a gentle voice that would not frighten them. We would tell them the bad dream is over and was never real and that the light has come. We would teach them the difference between sleeping and waking so that they could learn to call on the light. It is in this same way that we can awaken others with our forgiveness.

Perhaps someone has been treating us in an unloving manner, or worse yet, they may have been directly "attacking" us. The truth is, they are attacking us because, at that moment, they do not love themselves nor do they feel they are worthy of love from others. Their attacks are an asking for this love. When we are loving ourselves and feel we are worthy of love and respect, we do not treat people unlovingly. We do not attack. If we can quiet our anger and judgment, we will be able to see their desperate asking for love in that person's "attack" on us. The appropriate response, and a challenging one, is to offer them love.

This is what we were being taught when we were asked to love our enemies. We do not need to be reminded to love our friends or those who love us. This is easy to do. They are extending love to us. To love our enemies means to offer love to those who attack us, those who, rather than extending love, are calling for love. Everyone is either extending love or calling for love. Though it may appear very difficult to offer forgiveness, it is much less difficult than living with the unresolved anger and blame that constantly robs us of our peace of mind. To quote an old saying, "Resentment does more damage to the vessel in which it is stored, than to the object on which it is poured." Do we want revenge and resentment or peace and happiness? We cannot have both.

It is through our offering true forgiveness that we are "forgiven." By this I mean that we are reminded as to who we really are. If we understand their "attacks" are calls for love and healing, we will understand that about our "attacks." If we see another truly, we see ourselves through them as well. Another's "salvation" is our own. By remembering another's true sinless and guiltless nature and asking to see only this in another, we remind ourselves of our true nature. By freeing them from our judgments we are freeing ourselves. We cannot "forgive" ourselves until we are able to "forgive" others.

When someone behaves insanely, and all fearful behavior is insane, we can only heal or "correct" them by reminding them of their inherent sanity. We cannot do this by continually pointing out their insane behavior and judging it. By asking that we perceive them with complete unconditional love, we offer true forgiveness into the relationship. If we think for a minute how we would want others to react to us when we are acting fearfully, we will know how to react to others. When we are acting fearfully, we do not want someone to judge us or return our anger and fear. Rather we want them to calmly offer us love and compassion and remind us that our pain and fear will pass and our sanity will be restored.

Forgiveness is not a learned reaction. We cannot "learn" how to forgive. No matter how many books we read, thoughts we change, hours we meditate or pray, we cannot learn to forgive. Only God offers this true forgiveness through us. God offers His love through us. It is not learned, but is always complete and wholly perfect. This relieves us of the burden of learning and trying to forgive.

This is one of the most difficult things for us as humans to do. In reality, our egos cannot really offer this true forgiveness. We can only ask God to offer this through us. Whereas, our egos see the faults, God sees only the innocence and purity. We can bring our anger and judgment to God and ask that we be delivered from it. We can ask that the other's innocence be revealed to us. If we have only a "little willingness" to do this, even with the tumultuous emotions of anger, fear, and even hatred, He will offer us His forgiveness and peace. He will transform our thoughts of fear into ones of love.

A Call for Healing

This is the true message of the crucifixion, though we have used a fearful interpretation instead. Our fearful interpretation is that because we were such "sinners," Jesus had to die a painful death so that we might have the possibility of being saved from "eternal damnation" and offered "eternal life." This view insists that He died for our sins. This view makes the attacks on Him real and justifies the concepts of blame and sin. It serves to increase the guilt we feel and from which we must be freed to know God's peace.

There is another interpretation that is a far different view of the crucifixion, and that is viewed without fear or blame. Jesus was betrayed, abandoned, beaten, and finally killed though He harmed no one. He only spread a message of love and healed many. A close friend, Judas, "betrayed" Him. His disciples, whom He always loved and served, abandoned and denied Him. He was murdered in the most physically painful way known at the time. What greater "attacks" could a person experience than this?

But perhaps the crucifixion was intentionally created to teach us how to respond to "attacks." It effectively emphasizes that though the intensity of the assault of some children of God upon another appeared extreme, Jesus' reaction to that assault was to remind us that we should not give in to our temptation to respond with anger and counterattack.

As we observe Jesus' perceptions and responses to His attack, the message is clear. Before it occurred, He told His disciples it would happen and that they would betray Him. Yet, He did not reprimand them, but continued to love them unconditionally. He did not warn them of some inevitable punishment for their betrayal nor did He judge them for it. His awareness of His impending excruciating death did not frighten Him or cause Him to abandon His peace. When the attack occurred He asked the Father to forgive them because they had forgotten who they were and, therefore, did not know what they were doing.

Jesus is also reported to have said, "My God, My God, why have You forsaken me?" This too has been misunderstood. It was Jewish custom in those days to repeat the first words of a psalm, so as to recall the core concept. These words are the first words of Psalm 22. (Mysteriously, this Psalm, which occurs in the Old Testament written before Christ was born, speaks of oppressors who have "pierced my hands and feet" and "they divide my garments among them, and for my vesture they cast lots.") However, the writer of this Psalm goes on through his anguish to trust God and remember that He is "not far from me" and "will hasten to aid me." He closed with, "Let the coming generation be told of the Lord that they may proclaim to a people yet to be born the justice He has shown." Indeed, rather than a cry of being abandoned by God on the cross, Jesus was rather recalling Psalm 22, which is a statement of trust and belief in God.

Jesus did not "counterattack" though we would say he would have been "justified" in doing so. Three days later he arose to prove that the attack, and death, were not real. Only love is real. He died, not for our sins, but rather to demonstrate that attack and death are not real. The crucifixion was a call for peace and an example of the proper response to attack. By Jesus responding as He did to such a vicious attack, He offers us a model for our response, especially since attacks on us are seldom with such intensity.

Almost two thousand years later, another man, Martin Luther King, Jr., followed this example of responding to attackers with nonviolence of heart and deed. Like Jesus, he only asked that people accept and love each other, no matter what the color of their skin. After years of having violence and hatred directed at him from many people, he never forgot who they really were.

Before his tragic trip to Memphis, his aides pleaded with him not to go. There had been many death threats and the potential for violence was high. He decided to go anyway. He had felt for some time that his assassination was inevitable. It was just a matter of time.

That night he made a speech at a Memphis church. The end of the speech is quoted below. These are his last public words:

> It really doesn't matter what happens now. I left Atlanta this morning, and as we got started on the plane, there were six of us, the pilot said over the public address system, "We are sorry for the delay, but we have Dr. Martin Luther King on the plane. And to be sure all the bags are checked, and to be sure that nothing would go wrong with the plane, we had to check out everything carefully. And we've had the plane guarded all night."
>
> And then I got in to Memphis. And some began to say threats, and talk about the threats that were out. What would happen to me from some of our sick white brothers?
>
> Well, I don't know what will happen now. We've got some difficult days ahead. But it doesn't matter with me now. Because I've been to the mountaintop. And I don't mind. Like anybody, I would like to live a long life. Longevity has its place. But I am not concerned about that now. I just want to do God's will. And He's allowed me to go to the mountain. And I've looked over. And I've seen the promised land. I may not get there with you. But I want you to know tonight, that we, as a people, will get to the promised land. And I'm happy tonight. I'm not worried about anything. I'm not fearing any man. Mine eyes have seen the glory of the coming of the Lord.
>
> (From speech given on April 3, 1968, at the Bishop Charles Mason Temple, Memphis)

One comment symbolized how well he understood his "oppressor." He told his audience that there were death threats by "some of our sick white brothers." Those six simple words revealed a very clear and loving perception. By saying "some," he acknowledged that not all white people were mean-spirited. By referring to them as "sick," he reminded us that they were indeed sick and in need of healing, not "evil" and not in need of condemnation. Finally, by calling them "brothers," he reminded us of who we all are, always brothers and never enemies. The next morning he was shot and killed.

In many ways, the life of Martin Luther King, Jr., can be summed up in a statement read by Sir Richard Attenborough in the documentary *Mother Teresa* (1986):

> There is a light in this world. A healing spirit more powerful than any darkness we may encounter. We sometimes lose sight of this force because there is suffering, too much pain. Then suddenly, the spirit will emerge through the lives of ordinary people who hear a call and answer in extraordinary ways.

The Resistance to Forgiveness

Forgiving, in the true form, is so difficult for us that we often encounter strong resistance. It may be helpful to examine this resistance and our belief system concerning forgiveness. We are so wedded to the concepts of unjust treatment, justifiable anger, revenge, and retaliation, the martyrdom of forgiveness, etc., that we are often unable to see what a profound effect they are having on our marriages and relationships. When anyone even suggests that maybe we should consider loving and forgiving someone we are in conflict with, resistance will surface. This resistance encourages us to rationalize why we should not cease our counterattack and demand for retribution. In addition to our misperception of attack and sin by believing them to be real, there are certain other beliefs that block our decision to truly forgive.

FEAR THAT FORGIVENESS DICTATES A SPECIFIC ACTION: We may fear that to forgive may obligate us to continue in the relationship in a certain form, such as staying together or married when we may want to separate. We fear that should we forgive them we must remain married to them or physically with them. However, allowing ourselves to open our hearts and forgive someone we are in conflict with does not necessarily mean we are committed to remain physically or emotionally in the relationship in any particular form. In fact, the opposite is true. By keeping our hearts closed and resenting them, even if this is felt as even mild irritation, we are not completing our assigned lesson with them. The relationship has become rigid and stuck and we are not allowing the healing to occur so that we may move on, physically and/or emotionally. Even if we never see the other person again, or if they are dead, we are stuck and bound in that relationship until we have resolved all our unloving feelings. It continues to rob our peace of mind.

Allowing forgiveness to enter the relationship releases it. We have successfully completed our assignment and we will clearly perceive in what manner, if any, we are to remain in it. Even if the other person does not seem to be forgiving or affected by our forgiveness, we are freed in the relationship. Until we allow true forgiveness to enter for ourselves, even if the other chooses not to, it will not be clear to us how, and if, we are to proceed in the relationship.

Truly forgiving another person does not mean that we must continue in the relationship in any certain form. We may still decide to remove ourselves from the relationship physically. Forgiving does not mean that we will necessarily begin to love them in any certain way or even like them. Our goal is always to love them unconditionally, even if we desire a new form, such as that of an ex-mate. When we forgive someone, we may not begin to love them as a mate, or as a friend, or as a parent, etc., as perhaps we had once hoped we would. Now we love them as a Child of God. We have seen their inner purity, within their outer fearful form. This love is referred to as "agape," and reflects a more impersonal objective love for all mankind.

The other person may not resolve their own feelings of anger and attack. It is not necessary that they do for us to resolve our relationship with them. They are not yet willing to accept the gift of peace offered by true forgiveness. It is not even necessary that they be physically present in our lives, or even alive, for forgiveness and peace to enter. Many people fear that since they did not heal their relationship with someone before the person died, they will never find peace with that relationship. The ability to have peace and forgiveness enter any relationship is always open to us, no matter how great the perceived injustice, how ancient or extreme the hatred or how distant the person, even if they are no longer alive. Our ability to heal and restore peace to a relationship is always available to us, though we may choose not to accept or use it. We are not condemned to a lifetime of unresolved relationships.

FEAR THAT FORGIVENESS WILL CONDONE BEHAVIOR: Another fear is that if we forgive another, they will continue to "abuse" us or the relationship. Forgiving another does not mean allowing their fearful and attacking behavior to continue. Forgiving only means that we have pierced the illusion of this fearful behavior and understood it is a calling for love. In offering them the love they have sought, we may also decide that we do not want their offensive behavior to continue. We may need to approach them about this or remove ourselves physically. The difference now is that we do so from an awareness of love and understanding, not judgment and condemnation. We may decide that we need to physically leave the relationship if they remain unwilling to treat us lovingly. This may involve firmness without judgment. By making this essential shift in our minds, our subsequent actions, for which guidance will be given, may alter their behavior by offering them love and healing. Their initial or outward response may be anger, defensiveness, indignation, or attack. However, our love and our true forgiveness has created the miracle, and its effects, though sometimes unobservable, are sure.

FEAR THAT FORGIVENESS TAKES BOTH PEOPLE: Often we feel that we cannot change a painful, unhealed relationship if the other person does not want to change it as well. This fear is quite understandable, since we have been taught that it takes two to make a conflict, and therefore assume it must take two to resolve it. However, it only takes one—for that person. Peace can enter a relationship, at least for the person who has brought it from illusion to truth, from conflict to forgiveness.

We do not have control over, or responsibility for, another person's feelings and actions toward us. However, we do have both control and responsibility for how we choose to react toward their thoughts, feelings, and actions. By altering, and eventually mastering, our own thoughts and feelings in the relationship in order to extend love, we can then regain control over the effect the relationship has on us. We allowed the relationship to rule us by not controlling our thoughts and emotions, and therefore we can reverse the process. In doing so, we also give the other person greater freedom to truly be who they are.

FEAR THAT FORGIVENESS WILL NEGATE PUNISHMENT: We fear that without our retaliation, the other person will never get their deserved punishment and pain to counterbalance the "pain" they caused us. We need only remember that their attack was not real and they were never the cause of our pain. We may feel we are justified in withholding our forgiveness because we were once told "an eye for an eye and a tooth for a tooth." However, this statement was made to our species thousands of years ago, early in our spiritual development. It only asks that we do no greater harm to another than they did to us. If they took our eye, we should only take their eye, not an arm and leg also. If someone yells at us, we should yell back, not physically attack them, etc.

At that time we were not ready to "turn the other cheek" as we were later taught. "Turning the other cheek" was a major step for the species. This next concept of "true forgiveness" is the next and last major step. Until now, we also were not ready for this definition of forgiveness, whereby we recognize the "attack" never really occurred.

Other fears impinge on our ability to offer forgiveness. We fear that if we offer forgiveness, especially if the other person attacked first, it may appear that we are weak or cowardly. However, it is much braver to forgive than to attack. We fear that if we forgive it will indicate that the other person has been "right" all along and we have been "wrong." We may fear humiliation or the loss of esteem of others. However, the question need not be who is right or wrong, but rather how quickly can sanity be restored to the relationship. It is not the outcome that matters, but only how quickly can peace and love be restored, how much can we learn from each other.

These are some of the major fears that are in the way of our forgiveness. Though understandable, they are however inappropriate and unnecessary. We do not need to allow anything to block the healing that God has promised us. Our peace and joy will be found in our healed relationship, both with ourselves and others.

Chapter 9

The Period of Discomfort

$\mathcal{I}$t would be easy to assume that once you and your partner have united in a goal to transform your special relationship into a healed relationship, that serenity, joy, and clarity will now flood into your relationship and your life together will become clearer and less stressful than ever. In the long run, this is certainly true. You have turned in the direction of true love and joining. You have entered a path that is leading you toward the true and complete purpose of your relationship. Over time this serenity and joy will permeate the relationship and eventually will dominate it.

However, it must be understood that the transformation of an intense special relationship into a healed relationship is a process that may take many years. There is a period at the beginning of the transformation of a special relationship to a healed one that will be referred to as the period of discomfort. During this period the relationship is perceived as anything but joyful and peaceful, and may, in fact, seem less so than before. As with many physical healing processes, it may get more painful before it gets better. This is commonly accepted in holistic healing. Emerging from denial can often be initially painful.

Just as the major religious marriage vows mention, there is a holy purpose to marriage. However, it is not to take away the pain of our wounds, but rather to bring our wounds to the surface so that they can be healed. Remember that when we ask to love another unconditionally, we are asking that all our fears and wounds be revealed so that they may be healed. This healing occurs through the atmosphere of mutual understanding and forgiveness created by the budding healed relationship.

This does not mean that our immediate responses to the other's fearful behavior will always be a response of love and forgiveness. Often their fearful responses will trigger our fears. As these long repressed fears begin to surface, for a time they may put a great strain on the relationship. However, what is occurring in this emerging relationship is an understanding, once our upset has subsided, that our egos were reacting "insanely" and that is not who we truly are.

The healed relationship becomes a context that offers us the opportunity to reveal and heal our inner wounds.

The healed relationship becomes a context that offers us the opportunity to reveal and heal our inner wounds. As our wounds emerge, the relationship may appear combative, difficult, and stressful. The wounds will not be healed magically or effortlessly. These wounds keep us separate from others. As the healed relationship progresses, these wounds are healed. We then are released from our fears and our higher nature emerges. Assisting each other in healing these wounds and discovering and expressing this higher nature is the goal of the "healed relationship." Because of this, salvation and atonement (at-one-ment) are its true function.

In our "casual" special relationships, the period of discomfort may be much shorter, perhaps only minutes. Also, the intensity of this period may be in direct proportion to the ego's investment in the preexisting special love or hate relationship. In a casual relationship, this period may only appear as a brief period of awkwardness, perhaps as we offer a loving smile to a coworker we have previously ignored or resented. However, in our "major" special relationship we have erected an entire structure, an elaborate and complex way of relating to the other that must now change.

In a marriage or other "major" relationship, this period of discomfort can be very intense and confusing to both people. This is especially true if one or both were mistakenly expecting a period of tranquility. It is often during this period that one or both will decide to break off the relationship, though this is seldom necessary. If we understand the dynamics involved in this period of discomfort, we can more gently glide over this period and into the more peaceful later phases of the healed relationship.

The Darkest Hour Is Just Before Dawn

In addition to starting to reveal our wounds, there is another reason for this initial period of discomfort. It is that even though we have changed the "goal" of the relationship to one of joining and healing, we have not yet changed the structure of the relationship. In this context, the structure includes our entire way of thinking, feeling, behaving, talking, and relating together. This structure represents the day-to-day habits that have developed over the length of the relationship.

Previously the structure of the relationship was almost entirely ego-based. Each person was concerned primarily about whether their needs and goals were being met. This structure included the usual amount of judging and blaming ourselves and the other, along with its needed justification. For a period of time, this structure will remain in place even after a commitment is made to transform the relationship and its goals. In a beautiful moment of joining, in a holy instant, we have set on a new goal for the relationship. However, the ego, witnessing this brief moment of freedom, rushes to slam the prison gates closed again.

This period may introduce an element of awkwardness, and even distress, into the relationship as it becomes more and more apparent that the old, but still existing, structure does not suit the new goal. The new structure that will support this new goal has not yet developed. Even though we have committed to the new goal, old ego-based patterns of behavior and relating still rule on an everyday basis. We find ourselves arguing over the same perceived slights and injustices. We find the same judgments and condemnations creeping into our perceptions. We feel the same desire to seek another romantic relationship to fulfill all our needs.

Where before we had justified all this with our ego-based belief system, now we no longer feel as solid in our justification. Now we still have the same attack thoughts, but without the familiar, and much needed, justification. Our anxiety level increases. In addition we are becoming increasingly frustrated with our inability to reach our new goal of loving the other unconditionally. We are beginning to lack the faith that we and/or our mate can successfully fulfill the goal.

Before, when we blamed our mate or argued with them, we felt we were truly justified. Having believed we correctly analyzed their unloving behavior towards us, we were justified in attacking and correcting. After all, it was only self-defense and a desire to help that motivated us. Now, when we become judgmental or angry, we can no longer retreat to those justifications for consolation. Instead, what lays painfully revealed before us is our own unwillingness to love the other unconditionally. The pain may be more intense than that experienced in our "justifiable anger." It may become so intense that we will inevitably once again begin to blame the other, once again seeking to justify the special hate relationship. We believe that we could love them unconditionally, if only they were not so flawed!

The Purpose of the Period of Discomfort

Only a radical shift in purpose could trigger a complete change of mind as to what the relationship is for. And a complete change of mind is necessary to create a healed relationship. The goal of the relationship is abruptly shifted from getting to giving, from judging to loving. Before the ego's goal is what defined the meaning of the relationship. Without this goal, the relationship may temporarily seem to make no sense. Also the goals of the previous special relationship have not completely lost their attraction to us. For a period of time, the allure of the passion and cessation of loneliness promised by the special relationship may call to us. Even when we understand they are promises that, even if fulfilled, would still leave us unfulfilled, we may feel profound disappointment. We may feel anger that we may never have what we once believed we so dearly wanted, even needed, i.e., the special love relationship. Either due to our frustration at fully accomplishing a healed relationship, or our continued desire for a special relationship, we may decide to end our relationship in an attempt to reestablish another one, with the former goal of the special relationship. However, we do not need to leave the relationship.

There is a reason why the new commitment causes such an abrupt shift and distressful changes in the relationship. It is only in this way that the stark differences and contrast between the healed and special relationship can be made apparent. As these differences are made apparent it becomes clear that we have two choices. We can either decide to continue with the old, painful special relationship or to firmly commit to the new potentials and possibilities offered by the healed relationship, even if these are only a distant goal and hope now. We now have a clear view of our choices. We can either continue to attack and condemn our mate or we can choose to see their inner beauty and perfection. We can choose pain or peace.

The stark contrast between the two choices makes it clear that the available paths lead in two very different directions. As we view our existing relationship from the point of view of this new goal, we may even be appalled at our relationship's unclarity and selfishness. It may appear easy to retreat to the familiarity of the past relationship. However, the disruption of the change can only be solved by more change. This new goal of the healed relationship cannot coexist with the existing structure and form of the special relationship. They both contradict each other and one must give way to the other. Having once glimpsed Heaven, the previously tolerable hell is now intolerable.

Though it would be easy to dread this period of discomfort and bemoan its existence, it can be embraced. Though it does have its period of confusion and pain, as it progresses we will feel greater and greater levels of peace and happiness. We are freeing ourselves from fears that have influenced us for many years. The ego is beginning to lose sway over the relationship. Initially this is experienced as painful and disorienting, since it has been so thoroughly entrenched. However, in time the healing will be complete and the joy will emerge.

The Crisis of Faith

As this period of "discomfort" is entered, several dynamics begin to go to work. One of the first and most powerful is we begin to blame our partner for our distress. In addition, we are beginning to lose faith in their abilities to successfully transform the relationship with us. We focus on their mistakes, their lapses in commitment and clarity. We perceive them slipping into old unloving ways of relating to us (and themselves) and begin to wonder if they are truly capable of a higher way of relating. Their insecurities appear too deep, their vision too clouded. The judgment and anger we feel toward them may feel more intense than ever.

Actually, though we are projecting this anger and frustration onto our partner, it is really ourselves with whom we are angry and frustrated. We now know that we must offer our mate unconditional love and faith, but we are really angry at ourselves for being unable to do this. We are really questioning our own faith in accomplishing a healed relationship. To get rid of these feelings we project these onto the other and say it is really their fault that we are upset with them. We hope that we can remove this problem from its source and place it elsewhere. In truth, we do not need to feel this way toward ourselves or our mate.

During this period, we will lose faith as we are still in the developing stages of the new healed relationship. Do not be distressed when this happens. We need simply to ask that our faith be restored. Remember that every situation in which we find ourselves, every argument, every discussion is but a means to meet the new purpose set for our relationship. Spirit will use our special relationship to teach love. Our special relationship can become a teaching aid for our healed relationship.

We do not need to lack faith that the relationship can reach its goal. By trusting God to enter the relationship, we can trust that He will provide the means for its accomplishment. We must remember that it is God's will for every relationship that it be healed, so when we are losing faith in accomplishing this in our own relationship, we are losing faith in God's will. We do not have to bring the relationship to Him perfect, but only with a willingness to have Him purify it. No matter how difficult or even hopeless it may at times seem, we do not need to lose our faith, even though it may falter. We will make many mistakes along the way, but by holding to our commitment, our success is guaranteed. Since the goal of the healed relationship represents the true function that God has given it, every miracle needed for its fulfillment will be provided. It is not our ability to accomplish the goal that we are depending on, but God's.

This can be a very stressful and emotional period. The ego, feeling very threatened, will start to exert an even more intense influence. Since we have not totally released the old goal, not totally embraced the new goal, we may feel a sense of aimlessness in the relationship, which will be interpreted as stressful. We will reflect often on the former goal of the special relationship and wonder if perhaps it was really realizable, perhaps if we just tried a little harder and a little smarter, perhaps with a different partner. Though in truth our relationship has been saved, we may perceive it as having been lost.

Our lack of faith in our partner (and ourselves) may express itself in several forms. One common form is to remove from the relationship certain parts of it that are painful and to take these elsewhere to solve. We may decide that we can never communicate openly with our mate, so we avoid trying. We may discuss all our problems concerning the relationship with others, but not with our mate, fearing it will not be productive. We may decide that there are certain problems or issues that we simply cannot discuss with our mates. We may decide to seek sexual intimacy with another. In any and all of these cases, we feel we must "substitute" certain parts of the healed relationship.

Though we have rationalized this by determining that our mate is just incapable in certain areas, the decision actually reflects our lack of faith and our desire for withdrawal and avoidance. Nothing needs to be omitted from the healed relationship. No matter what we judged our and our partner's capabilities to be before we joined in a healed relationship, all that has changed now. God has entered the relationship and His capabilities are limitless. Be patient.

Usually many years are involved in transforming the special love/hate relationships that comprise most marriages into the healed union. And we are not a patient society. I do not mean to place limits on how quickly all this can progress. Indeed some people may sail through the period of discomfort or even avoid it entirely. On the other hand, for most of us the transition will appear somewhat lengthy, as the ego is slow to give up its turf. We have heard many people say that a marriage is hard work, and applying the principles outlined in this book does take hard work, with ourselves and with our relationship. Perhaps if we knew how hard it would be, we would be reluctant to marry in the first place. It may appear "easier" to live alone, but the opportunities for self-growth, and therefore greater freedom and joy, can be limited in a solitary life.

However, do not be disheartened by what appears to be a lengthy and laborious process. Though we may not have consciously recognized it as yet, we have been seeking this process our whole life. Once we have discovered the location (the healed relationship) of what we have sought (peace and joy), we may feel frustrated to learn that it may take years to reach.

This does not mean that we have to endure many years of suffering before we finally find the joy and peace we are seeking. Actually, trapped in our special relationship, we have already endured much of our suffering. As soon as we begin our journey toward the healed relationship, we have begun to free ourselves, and our suffering will begin to abate and our joy will begin to increase. We have finished with dead-ends and are once again on the road Home. However, the road to the total peace and joy we have always felt was possible may seem to be a long one and we must be patient or we will lose heart, though even this is only temporary.

We must remember that if we truly want the goal of peace and happiness that the healed relationship can offer us, we must be willing to use the only means that will deliver us to this happy end. The means is our true forgiveness of the other and our continuing choice to see them as sinless and flawless, to see them through the eyes of love. As long as we continue to choose to judge and condemn, we may say we want the end, but we are not ready to use the means. Our asking for God's help, no matter how muddled or weak the request, makes this goal possible and guaranteed.

We probably never thought it would take so much time, so much work, so much vigilance to our thoughts and emotions, as it does to create a truly clear and healed relationship. But it does. For generations the ego's ancient hold on this world has been tenacious. However, it is quickly losing its grip. We need to be patient with ourselves and others. If our commitment to the goal continues, even if at times it fades or seems to be lost, we have been assured we will accomplish the goal. It is not through the strength of our egos that this will be accomplished but through the strength of the Spirit within us.

Chapter 10

Arguments as a Teaching Aid

*R*ecently, I was in a dispute with a business colleague who was also a friend. I was sure I was legally, as well as ethically, in the right. Everyone on "my team" agreed wholeheartedly. Even my lawyer said I was legally right, and that any court would side with me. "Don't let her get away with it!" we shouted. "Defeat her. She deserves it! Go for the win!" The conflict had lasted several months and was coming to a head. The other person was avoiding my attempts to contact her, anticipating an argument that she would probably lose. I was looking forward to the battle as I was sure I would win. As I was discussing how right I was with another friend, he said, "Robert, remember it is not the outcome that matters."

These nine words reminded me of the loving way to view the conflict. It stopped my planned attack dead in its tracks, much to the amazement of my supporters, all of whom were looking forward to a win. Until then, the victorious outcome was all we had been focusing on. My friend's comment reminded me of the truth about the situation. I remembered we were being brought together in this conflict not to have one triumph over the other, but rather to teach and learn love from each other. That was the only standard by which to measure the interaction's success.

I gave up all desire to "win" (well, almost all) and wanted only to heal our relationship. I asked myself, "What would bring peace in this situation?" When I finally reached her on the phone, I said, "I have been thinking for days how to start this discussion. What I want to say to you to set the tone is: My lovely sister, what can we learn from each other today?" She audibly relaxed. Having experienced an attack, her defenses were solidly in place. They immediately were lowered. After an hour-long discussion, all matters were settled fairly and amicably. Though we still disagreed on several areas, we agreed to disagree. Both of us found a resolution we could both live with. There was no winner, no loser.

This is another way to perceive arguments and conflicts. During this "period of discomfort" there will be many opportunities to enhance our commitment to our goal of deeper joining. These opportunities will often present themselves in the form of arguments with our mates. These arguments can be used to reveal our wounds and barriers that prevent us from loving and joining. In this way they can be seen as teaching aids for the emerging healed relationship.

Recently in a small workshop, a woman in her forties was sharing her thoughts and feelings about her anticipated next relationship. She had been married twice and the relationships ended painfully. She was both looking forward to another relationship and yet also fearful that it too would end in arguments, pain, and separation. She was determined not to argue in the next relationship. At one point, she shared, "I just hope I am together enough now so that we do not argue. I really want a clear relationship, just harmony and peace."

This may be possible for a few people, but for most of us arguments are a necessary and healthy part of any marital relationship. For arguments to be a healthy part, we need only to change our perception of our arguments. We must begin to perceive that marriage will reveal our wounds and that, until those are healed, our initial response upon revealing a wound will often be anger. It is this anger, projected onto another, that leads to the arguments. Healthy marriages can include arguments that are perceived as teaching aids. Arguments are teaching aids in our learning to love unconditionally, nothing more but nothing less.

However, most marital arguments are perceived as skirmishes on the ongoing battlefield of the relationship. Here arguments are perceived as weapons, not teaching aids. The objective is not growth and learning, but rather victory. We enter another battle hoping that just maybe in this skirmish our mate will finally understand how wrong they have been all these years. Then maybe, finally, once they see this, we can have the peaceful, loving relationship we have always sought. This "logic" (and I use this word loosely) assumes that if we can finally "defeat" our "opponent" by proving we are right and they are wrong, we will have peace. All of us know there is never a real or lasting peace produced when one party has defeated another. There is only resentment and hatred. True peace comes only from the clear understanding, and valuing, of the different perspectives of all parties involved and then mutually deciding on solutions that everyone can support.

An Example of "Arguments as Weapons"

Recently Julia and I were counseling a couple, let us call them Paul and Sandy, who were nearing divorce after twenty-four years of marriage. Their marriage had reached the stage of deep hostility and severe dysfunction. The degree of the family crisis was demonstrated by the acting out of self-destructive behavior by two of the five children. As each one talked to us, their main aim was to convince us, and their mate, of how most, if not all, of their problems were the fault of the other person. Each one was very convincing, being absolutely convinced themselves. If they could convince us, this would be further "proof" they were right. Convincing us could be a great weapon in their arsenal. "See, even they thought you were wrong." That could be major artillery. It was clear that both were right and both were wrong, neither was right and neither was wrong.

The wife told of problem after problem "caused" by the husband's more passive, lenient behavior. Sandy explained that she was the source of the ambition and financial stability in the family, as Paul was less motivated and more easygoing. She perceived the children's problems as the result of his more undisciplined, lenient parenting style. She explained how the children all wanted to live with him after the divorce, as he was easier on them and she was forced to be the disciplinarian. She perceived he had "bribed" them to love him more. She said she was forced to be stricter with the children to make up for his lack of discipline. She felt he was too lenient, too easygoing, too unmotivated, too undisciplined, too unconcerned with the children.

When Paul spoke he told of his wife's drive to accomplish and own. He explained how she had little time for him or the children and that he felt obligated to offer the children constant support and love to offset her strict and inattentive behavior. He perceived the children's problems as being "caused" by her distant and strict behavior towards them. He agreed that his ambitions were less and felt that was an asset, not a liability. He felt she was wrong for being too driven, too strict, too hard, too motivated, too concerned with business and money.

What had gone wrong here was obvious. Each had stopped respecting and honoring the differences between them that had first attracted them to each other and that could have provided for an excellent balance in the relationship. Paul's easygoing, lenient approach could have merged well with Sandy's more aggressive, determined manner to create a well-balanced and harmonious relationship and family. Each could have provided what the other one "lacked" and the positive sides of each person's nature would have been accentuated. However, instead of honoring these differences in their natures, they began to judge them and decide that their way was better and the other's was worse. Instead of honoring, they began to fight the basic differences in each other's nature. They began to demand that their mate severely alter their basic nature and way of being in the world. This is something no one can, or should, ever do. As the conflict progresses, the negative aspects of their natures began to become more predominant.

As they continued to judge each other over the years, the differences in their natures became more extreme. Instead of becoming less driven and authoritarian, Sandy felt it necessary to become more so to "fight" against Paul's "flawed" nature. Instead of Paul becoming more disciplined and motivated, he became less, as a response to her heightened judgment and aggressive, domineering behavior. Each one was "right" in their evaluation that there were negative aspects to the other's nature. Each one was "right" and could clearly see how these negative aspects were having a detrimental effect on the relationship and children. However, what they had failed to understand was that it was their perception of the differences in their natures that was really causing the conflict. They also could not see that it was their conflict, not their inherent differences, that was taking a toll on the children.

Had their arguments over the years been used as teaching aids instead of battles, they could have learned to respect these differences. No one can really change their basic nature. Sandy would always be more ambitious and disciplined. Paul would always be more easygoing and lenient. However, had the arguments been perceived differently, each could have assisted the other in accentuating the positive parts of their nature while minimizing the negative. Instead the opposite occurred.

Had the arguments been used as teaching aids, their perception of the relationship and each other would be quite different. They could have sat with us as a happy couple with well-adjusted children and described their relationship and their differences quite differently. He may have said, "You know, I am much less disciplined or motivated than Sandy, and even though this has caused conflict at times, she really has helped me to organize my life and to accomplish a lot of things I was only dreaming about before. Also, I really appreciate her desire and ability to create financial abundance. It makes a lot of things easier. Though she still comes up with most of the rules for our children regarding study habits, chores, personal habits, etc., I support these and I am glad it is important to her. Otherwise, if I was in charge of the rules I think our children, though feeling loved, would lack good work habits and self-discipline."

Sandy's view of the differences, after years of using arguments as teaching aids instead of weapons, may have gone quite differently as well. "Since I was brought up to think that the man should always be more ambitious, after awhile Paul's easygoing nature really bothered me. I was trained to think that the man would take care of me and the children financially. However, after many conflicts I finally realized that I was indeed much more motivated towards business than many women and that I enjoyed business as well as parenting. I realized that even though Paul did not fit my preconceived pictures of a 'normal' man in this area, neither did I fit the picture of a 'normal' woman. I finally realized Paul's 'enjoy every day' attitude was a nice balance. It has made me slow down and relax instead of always working towards some future goal. If he had not added that element into our family, I think our children, though highly motivated and accomplished, may have felt of value only for what they do, not for who they are. We all have a lot more fun because of Paul."

The battlefield of their relationship had created none of the positive benefits they had longed for. They were unhappy together and tortured by their constant judgment and attacks on each other. The battles had begun to wear on their health. For the most part their children were neither well motivated nor self-disciplined. Nor did they exhibit a sense of self-worth or enjoyment of life reflecting a sense of being loved unconditionally. Years of using "arguments-as-weapons" had taken its toll. A change of perspective, to begin to view arguments as teaching aids, can stop any further damage and begin to correct many of the existing problems.

It May Get Worse Before It Gets Better

Even after we commit to a healed relationship, arguments will continue. As before, there will be annoyances, differences, and major blowups. During this period, the arguments may become more intense than ever. In the past we have always attempted to settle these by proving we are right and our partner wrong. We have believed that there was something to win on the battlefield. We have reverted to detailed discussions of each person's emotional problems in an attempt to explain their "flaws" and unconscious behavior. We rationalize, "If only our mate would truly see their flaws and change them, then this relationship would work." We then either leave the battlefield victoriously or defeated or in an unstable truce. Usually these results offer little real growth and understanding and even less peace. Often we do not truly desire peace, but rather victory on the battlefield of our relationship.

Also, we can try different processes for resolving our arguments with each other. First, we must change our perspective of our arguments. We must let go of our perspective of viewing "arguments-as-weapons" to be used towards our victory on the battleground of our relationship, and begin to perceive them as teaching aids. When our arguments occur, it is because we have once again revealed an unhealed wound. This then gives us one more opportunity to understand the wound and heal it.

When Sandy expressed her frustration with Paul's lack of motivation and discipline, this could have offered him the opportunity to see if he had any blocks to being motivated and disciplined. Sandy could have used the argument to examine her desire to have him be more like her, her need to accomplish and own, and her blocks to loving Paul unconditionally. When Paul was exasperated by Sandy's aggressive, authoritarian nature, this could have given Sandy a chance to examine her need to control and achieve, while at the same time offering Paul the opportunity to examine his fears to expressing his will and his blocks to loving Sandy unconditionally.

This change in perception can also lead to a change in response and action. During our attacks and our arguments, our common goal to joining will seem very distant. Even though it seems distant, it is not. The goal of joining is immediately available to us if we are willing to allow it back in. We need only to cease our attack, our explanations, and even our attempts to resolve the issue by our own efforts, and once again offer the problem in particular, and the relationship in its entirety, over to God. We need only ask that we see the other through the eyes of unconditional love (God). We must ask ourselves, "What will bring peace here?" We must ask ourselves if we would rather be right or happy.

We need to stop our argument as soon as we can, and even though we may still be angry and fearful, offer our willingness to have God restore peace to our relationship. One or both people can sit quietly and turn within and ask that peace be restored. We may need to wait for a cooling off period after the arguments for our fears and anger to subside. Even though we may feel wounded, justifiably angry, and absolutely right, simply realize that we do not know how to bring peace to our relationship, but Spirit does. Emotional and mental clarity is not required for healing, only a little willingness. God does not demand that we remove all guilt, anger, and fear from our minds. That is Spirit's function.

Sometimes, the way Spirit will resolve these issues is quite unusual, even comical. Such a situation occurred recently between my wife, Julia, and myself. We found ourselves in one of those arguments where I was sure she was wrong and she was sure I was wrong. We had been on the battlefield for about an hour with no clear "winner" (even the "winner" is the loser). As we were arguing, the phone rang. Since neither of us was in any mood to talk to anyone, we lapsed into silence as the phone rang several times before the answering machine finally answered. During this pause, I halfheartedly asked to see her through God's eyes, even though I was sure even God thought she was wrong and was mad at her too. As we waited, fuming silently, for the caller to leave his message, a miracle occurred. The caller was my childhood friend, Harley. Harley is a musician and he always sings a little song to the machine, in a comical Southern twang, if I am not at home. As we quietly listened, he began to sing "I Can See Clearly Now, the Rain Has Gone" in his heavy Southern accent. Both of us could not help but laugh at the comic relief and the clarity of the message. Habit caused us to continue the argument for a few minutes after the call, but it had lost its fervor. Soon we both stopped trying to make each other wrong, listened to each other's perception, and agreed to work towards a solution. We were both able to observe what an investment we had in being right and how this blocked our love for each other. Peace was soon restored to our relationship.

Only the Process Matters, Not the Outcome

In a healed relationship, we begin to understand it is not the outcome of an argument that matters. The only thing that matters is the process. It is not important who was right and who was wrong or who hurt whom the most. It does not matter who started the argument in the first place. To determine if the "argument" served its purpose as a teaching aid in establishing the healed relationship, we need to ask ourselves certain questions. What have we learned through the interaction? Did we teach and learn love or fear? Were we able to better understand our wounds that made us decide to attack or counterattack? Did we learn to love each other more? Were we able to see their beauty or only their flaws? Has the relationship become more healed or more fearful? Did we help remind each other of who we truly are or did we help each other forget? What have we learned of our own barriers to love? Rather than changing the other, have we changed ourselves?

Having now established a goal of a healed relationship, we may still want to bring our upset to our mate, but not as a weapon of attack, blame, or condemnation. Instead, we understand the we are responsible for our emotions and are only temporarily acting insane by blaming them. Our intention is to use our partner's greater clarity (sanity) at the same time to rescue us from our insanity by their seeing through it to our inner light. We can say, "I am very angry with you and blaming you. I know this is just my temporary insanity, but I need to tell you what I am feeling so we can lead each other back to our sanity." Whichever one of us is saner at the time the argument occurs can remember how deep our indebtedness is to the other for revealing love and our barriers to it.

A Biological Basis for Arguments?

Recent research on marriage arguments has revealed some fascinating data that may indicate that a certain level of arguments between the sexes is unavoidable. However, understanding this information may help us understand our mate's reactions during arguments. It seems that the "flight or fight" mechanisms and emotions for the male are more fully triggered when they feel criticized or attacked. When criticized or verbally attacked (there is no difference between the two), their physiological (blood pressure, heart rate, etc.) and psychological responses are more strongly engaged than a woman's and remain distressed for a longer period of time, often long after their mates have calmed down. Therefore, a man's emotional response to criticism or anger, say from his mate, is often overwhelming to him and he may explode or retreat or "stonewall," which is to not respond until he "has a handle on his emotions." Often a woman will not understand his strong responses.

On the other hand, a woman usually responds more strongly to this stonewalling, this withdrawal and refusal to interact, than a man would in a similar situation. Unwillingness to immediately respond triggers unpleasant psychological and physiological responses in her. Someone shutting down until they can "think through" their emotions is often much more upsetting to a woman than it would be to a man. She may perceive this unresponsiveness as insulting or as an unwillingness to look at the issue.

So, we have this crazy cycle of a man getting criticized, then overreacting and stonewalling, and then the woman overreacts to this stonewalling and criticizing more and the man stonewalls more and on and on until the cycle is broken. These gender-related responses can create a cycle of arguing as each person's response triggers the other's upset. If the cycles are not understood and broken, they can destroy the marriage, and often the physical health of the partners as well. However, all this arguing can also be used as a teaching aid for love.

Recent research concerning stressful marriages has also shown a surprisingly accurate correlation of positive interaction to negative ones. It seems if a five to one ratio of positive to negative interactions exists (five positive to every one negative), the marriage is usually successful as described by its participants. In other words, we can tolerate a little negative if there is a lot of positive. The good moments of mutual support, pleasure, passion, caring, etc., must outnumber the "bad" moments of conflict, coldness, anger, etc., by five to one. With "volatile" couples they may need twenty-five positive experiences to offset their five arguments each week. A more "compatible" couple may need only five positive to offset their one argument.

Also, if during arguments a couple will use certain "cooling down" statements, these can effectively de-escalate the argument and allow it to end or to proceed without contempt or vindictiveness. These are statements such as, "I know I do that too," "You do not do that all the time," "I know I am very sensitive on that issue," "I really love our relationship, but this makes me crazy," "I may be wrong, I often am." These statements add a moment of sanity into an insane situation.

Resolving Arguments

An argument is not resolved if we finish the argument feeling one person was "right" and the other "wrong." Whether we agree or disagree on who was right or wrong does not matter. It does not matter who went insane first, who was more insane, or how the different forms of insanity expressed themselves. Arguing is a form of insanity because it reflects the illusion that the other's fearful behavior is who they really are. Arguments are a manifestation of our insanity because they reflect our insane belief in our separation. Unless we remember that all forms of anger, blame, resentment, and condemnation are forms of insanity, which need healing, not condemnation and punishment, then we have not yet understood the nature and the purpose of the argument. It will just appear again in another form, at another time.

If we leave the argument mutually deciding that certain behavior changes would create greater peace in the relationship, this can be helpful. If we leave the argument with greater clarity as to the roots of our insane perceptions and the blocks to our love, this can be healing and freeing. However, if we leave the argument feeling one was right and the other wrong, we have just solidified our fears. We have reinforced a belief system that we are all separate egos, some better than others. We have failed to perceive the call for love hidden within the attack. We have added to the unclarity that created the argument to begin with. This "resolution" is only a temporary rest. More arguments will follow as the illusion has been given greater "reality."

An argument is only truly resolved when we recognize that we both went temporarily insane and forgot who we were. True resolution comes with the understanding that no one was wrong and no one was right. Though our insanity may appear quite different, one may shout, the other sullenly withdrawn, it was still a form of insanity. One person may appear to be justified since the other "started it." It was still insanity. For the argument to be truly resolved, and we must both understand and accept that we were insane or we would not have decided to attack or counter-attack. When this is done, the argument is complete, there is no wound left open, no "record of wrong," no solidifying the illusion that someone was "flawed." Now the argument has been used as a teaching aid to teach love and the healed relationship.

An argument is only truly resolved when we recognize that we both went temporarily insane and forgot who we were.

This process will be repeated many times. The goal of the healed relationship will need to be continually renewed as it develops into a constant and bright light at the center of the relationship. These arguments can become a source of frustration and even lead to a sense of hopelessness. Will we ever be able to stop judging others and just love them unconditionally all the time? Will the arguing ever stop? Probably not as long as we still have a body and an ego.

However, we can begin to change our perception of arguments and understand they are a component of most healthy relationships and can be used as teaching aids. Since our relationship's function is to expose to us the barriers we have to love, and since those barriers are always our wounds, our unhealed perceptions, exposing these wounds will always involve a certain amount of anger (and, therefore, arguments) as we move towards healing. We can give each other permission to "go temporarily insane" and attack and blame. We can agree to never take any argument personally, because no matter how it may seem, the other person is not upset for the reasons they think. It is themselves they are angry at, not us. These arguments have then become useful in revealing our barriers to love, so that they can become more quickly released.

We can continue to offer our anger and judgment to Spirit when it arises. We can strive to remember that all arguments and judgments can be transformed into a teaching aid to be used to demonstrate the healed relationship. The healed relationship is a process, a state of striving. We are evolving a new paradigm in human relationships and it will not be easy. But remember we are slowly transforming the thought-forms that have evolved in our species over millennia. As we continue to do this, the true beauty and clarity of the healed relationship will continue to emerge.

Correcting Others: An Exercise in Futility

If we really want to see what would be most effective to help another through their fears, we need only ask what would be the best way to wake a child from a bad dream. After all, when we are fearful, we are just children having a nightmare. We think the fear (bad dream) is real, but it is not. We mistakenly believe that someone has hurt us, or that something awful has happened, or that we are not lovable, or that something terrible might happen, etc. We are just dreaming a bad dream and need to be awakened from it.

When a child is tossing and turning in a bad dream, it is not best to shake them suddenly out of it and then tell them it is ridiculous for them to be scared of a dream that obviously is not real. Rather, it is best to gently awaken them and remind them that your love is real and you are there with them and they are safe. Often no reference to the night-mare is even needed.

We can use this technique to rouse our mates from the bad dream of their fears. Rather than suddenly awakening them with our attacks, corrections, and criticisms, we can gently stroke them awake with our love. Rather than telling them they are foolish for even believing in the night-mare, we can simply remind them that our love is real and they are safe. This technique works best for children of all ages, from one to one hundred.

Usually in our marital relationships we feel we must uncover, judge, and then correct our mate's flaws and insecurities. We fear that if we do not correct others, they will just continue in their unloving ways and certainly that would not be fair! If they do not change, we must continue to suffer in the wake of their thoughtless and unkind behavior. We then decide that their unloving feelings and acts that we were victim to must be corrected or else our relationship in particular, and the planet in general, will never progress. We must correct them. We decide that it is our duty to point out our mate's flaws for their own good, so they can become aware of them and grow. It is only fair. To our egos this seems kind and right. We then offer this correction to "better" the relationship, not realizing we are doing just the opposite.

Usually, the person and relationship does not seem to get better through our continual correcting. Constantly judging and drawing attention to another's flaws does not usually result in their "correction." We are always hoping they will say, "Ah! Thank you for pointing out my insecurities and unloving behavior. I really had not noticed it or understood it until now. Now that you have so wisely made me aware of it, I will resolve it as soon as I can so that it will not affect us or our relationship again." Do we know of anyone who has even come close to making that statement when they were corrected?

In fact, our corrections often seem to solidify and even amplify their insecurities. This is because it is almost inevitable that our pointing out their flaws is laced with our feelings of attack and judgment. After all, we feel justified to counterattack or correct. We also believe that if we were attacked first, then our counterattack is totally justified. If our mate yells at us in anger, then our yelling back is only a response to their initiating the attack. Our attack is totally justified. In fact, they are the cause of our attack, so they are to blame for both their attack and our counterattack. We then feel we are not responsible for our counterattack, they are.

Indeed, we may be "right" from the ego's point of view in our estimation of their "flaws" and unloving behavior. We may be morally, ethically, and logistically correct. We can even get others to agree that indeed what someone did to us was indeed unfair, inconsiderate, unloving, unconscious, contemptuous, etc., etc., etc. In fact, the more agreement we can muster, the surer we become that we are right and the other wrong. Sound familiar? The problem here is that even when we are right, we are wrong.

At best our "wise and perceptive" understanding of their insecurities may result in their agreement that they are indeed "wrong" and we are right. Now, believing themselves wrong or flawed, they believe even more in their inherent unworthiness, which is the wellspring of their unconscious behavior to begin with. Usually, after our angry counterattack, either covert or overt, we often feel depressed. Even if successful, our attempts to convince them of how wrong they are (and how right we are) do not result in joy and joining. The result is not greater happiness and peace for either. The question we must ask ourselves is, "Would we rather be right or happy?" Many times we would rather be right.

The reason that drawing attention to the "flaws" or insecurities of others does not help is that we have no way of knowing when they are ready to look at the fears that are causing these insecurities. And until someone is ready to understand and release their fears, nothing we say will be of any value. In fact our bringing these issues to light only seems to upset them. Usually anger will be their response, just as anger is the response of anyone we try to wake up before they are ready to awaken.

We do not need to point out their problems nor do we need to worry when and how they will be corrected. At the exact instant someone is ready to see their fears, they will. We do not have to be concerned when they will understand them or how. They will be brought the information as soon as they are ready to understand it and in a manner that they are most willing and able to hear it.

Often, our mates will not choose us to be the teachers of certain lessons, even though we would very much like to be. Instead, they may precipitate an incident, read a book, overhear a conversation, hear something on a talk show, or just have an inner realization that will serve as a teaching aid. When they are ready to observe and release a fear, they will create the perfect mechanism so that they can most easily and effectively do so. They will choose a teaching aid that is most appropriate for their level of understanding. We never know what this will be, but we can be sure it is almost never their mate judgmentally pointing out the fear.

The Relationship as a Safe Haven

How then can we help others observe and release their fears so that they will no longer negatively effect our relationship? If you ask yourself what type of relationship, what type of atmosphere, is most conducive for us to look at our fears, we will have the answer. Rather than an environment of constant criticism and correcting, it is rather an environment of unconditional love and acceptance.

By deciding to offer our mates, and others, unconditional love, our relationships and our homes become a place of deep rest. Here, perhaps as no other place in our lives, they can feel totally accepted and loved, just as they are, faults and all. Let others point out our mate's flaws. There are many other people who will gladly fill that role. But we can choose to offer love. We need to be love finders, not fault finders.

It is in this type of supportive, loving environment that they are most willing to begin to examine their fears and insecurities. They feel safe and loved. They may feel free to ask our opinion and advice about their problems, as they never did before in an environment of judgment and condemnation. However, now they are asking us to explore the roots of their fears with them. This is quite different from our suggesting or demanding that they explore them. By asking, they have indicated that they are both ready and have chosen us to help.

The relationship will become a "safe home" where each person is striving to remind the other of who they really are.

Within this safe haven, they will be aware that we are always attempting, though not always successfully, to see the "spiritual perfection," rather than making their fears "real." The relationship will become a "safe home" where each person is striving to remind the other of who they really are. Integrated into our relationship will be the awareness that we all act insanely, it just expresses itself differently. Part of this insanity is being sure that another's insanity is much worse than our own. By remembering that we all are inherently sane, we can choose to view another's "mistakes" from a loving perspective. Though often difficult to do, this, rather than pointing to their flaws, is the most effective way to assist in another's healing. This is a healed relationship.

Somebody Stop Me!

Within this healed relationship we may still request that our mates change certain behavior, but we are not saying that they are flawed. For instance, we may tell our mates that we need help with the household chores or that we would like them to talk with us more or to stop treating us inconsiderately. These are requests for behavioral changes, not corrections of perceived flaws.

Many years ago, Julia requested a change of behavior that literally changed my life. At that time I was totally involved in a business venture that was taking almost all of our time, energy, and money. She was working with me and was equally involved and drained. Since our younger daughter, Alicia, was not around yet and our older daughter, Julie, was a teenager, it seemed the appropriate time for a total commitment to business.

As often happens with start-up businesses, we seemed to always be in crisis. We were working ten- to fourteen-hour days with no real relief in sight. Being your basic type A overachiever, I did not really mind the strain, even though it was taking its toll. Julia hated it. After one particularly stressful week, Julia asked me a key question: "Is this the way you always want your life to be?" she asked nonjudgmentally. "Because if it is, I am not sure I want to be in it."

Her lack of real criticism allowed me to hear the question without defenses. She simply wanted to know the answer, so that she could decide. That comment stopped me in my tracks. It was not just that I did not want to separate but also the realization that another approach to the dilemma might be possible. I had just assumed that this level of intensity, this willingness to have everything out of balance in the name of success, was required. I realized that, though at times it was exhilarating and satisfying, basically this lifestyle was exhausting and depleting and doing damage in key family relationships.

After giving her question some soul-searching thought, I told her that I too did not want this lifestyle. I knew it was crazy, but I did not know how to stop it. I just needed someone to remind me I did not need to keep doing this. We then agreed that, instead of every decision being based on my fear as to whether the business would succeed or not, we would allow another factor to enter in. We began to make decisions that we felt would lead us to greater peace, ones that would restore balance to our lives.

It took several years for our lifestyle to regain its balance and peace. We know the results would not be instantaneous. We were inheriting many years of unconscious momentum. However, we both now had a common goal and were of one mind in our purpose. Sometime later we saw a scene in a movie that we felt comically brought home the concept that at times somebody just needs to stop us and tell us to stop acting so crazy. The movie was *The Mask,* a comedy about a mild-mannered, shy bank clerk who finds an ancient mask. Whenever he puts on the mask, all his inhibitions drop away and his crazy side emerges. He becomes an outrageous playboy. One night he puts on the mask and before he leaves his apartment he looks in the mirror. With a devilish grin of total mischievousness, he says, "Somebody stop me!" Julia and I have come to use that image and expression in our relationship, as well as other relationships, whenever we feel one of us is getting too crazy and we need someone to stop us.

It is the lack of judgment, and the realization that someone can stop acting "crazy," that allows us to ask for changes without correcting or criticizing. The other person can call us to a higher level of awareness, to our true self. We must observe our own motivation and, as much as possible, release our judgment and just try to explain what our needs are in the situation. The key here is what is really in our hearts. If the request is just a cleverly disguised attack, they will respond defensively and no healing will occur. At first they may interpret these requests as corrections and react accordingly (anger, defense, withdrawal, etc.). If the request is simply a suggested change in behavior, knowing that this desired change does not imply a flaw in the character or the "reality" of an attack, then, at some level, it will be heard as such and healing will begin.

This is very difficult to do. Usually our first, and often sustained, response when confronted with others' attacking or fearful behavior is to defend, counterattack, and correct. In the middle of the argument, it may prove too difficult for us to offer our unconditional love. We may need to leave the battlefield and again ask Spirit to transform these feelings and to use our argument as a teaching aid to teach love. It may take us some time to feel this way and our initial attempts to love, while we are still angry, may feel insincere or hypocritical. This is to be expected and we may need to just keep working with our feelings until we feel our peace being restored. Though it may appear much more difficult to continue to offer unconditional love in the face of someone's ongoing unloving behavior, this is the only path that can truly heal their minds from the fear that they are guilty and, therefore, unlovable. It is only this fear that created the behavior to begin with.

We must be gentle and patient with ourselves, as well as with another. We will still get angry, attack, and try to correct. We will not always be able to offer another unconditional love. We do not need to condemn ourselves when we are not responding lovingly. The creation of a healed relationship does not require perfection. Rather, it only asks that we continue to recommit to this goal, once balance and perspective have been restored. A healthy relationship allows for both people to go temporarily insane, often at the same time.

Chapter 11

Separation and Divorce:
A Change of Form

*T*hough "till death us do part" is written in many marriage vows, it is not inherent to all marriages that they must last a lifetime for them to be successful and complete. In the past, most marriages did last a lifetime. Average life spans were forty to fifty years, so marriages only needed to last twenty or thirty years. Now their duration can be fifty to seventy years. In the past, economic realities and social and religious structure discouraged divorce and allowed few options except staying together. Also, society and people changed very little in past generations. The person you were when you married was very similar to the person you were when you died. All this has changed in Western societies in the last fifty years.

Divorce is always upsetting and every attempt should be made to "save" the marriage. Especially if children are involved, divorce can destroy the sense of security that the marriage is meant to provide. All too often people give up on the union long before they even understand the forces that are making it painful or unfulfilling for them. Often this is because the marriage is revealing our unhealed wounds. Actually, this revealing of wounds is a healthy function of the marriage, but can become so painful that we may project our anger and blame onto our mate and/or flee the relationship. Often, if the real reasons that the relationship is not working are understood, the issues can be solved and the relationship healed.

However, not all marriages can or should be saved. A union has not failed because it has not endured a lifetime. Physically staying in a toxic relationship can drain our spirit and undermine our health. At times, leaving the relationship may be the most loving and courageous path toward peace. Divorce or separation is not an indication that the relationship was a "mistake" and should never have happened. The relationship in its mated form, and in its separated form, was perfect. Both people came together to learn from each other and from the different forms of the relationship, exactly what they were meant to learn.

Just as there are conscious and unconscious marriages, so are there conscious and unconscious divorces. As with marriages, an unconscious divorce is primarily motivated by fear and illusion (an unhealed divorce); a conscious divorce is primarily motivated by love and truth (a healed divorce). A conscious divorce is one in which the reasons for separating are clear and the striving to love the other unconditionally continues, but in a different form. This clarity is often reached after the fact.

An unconscious divorce is one where the real reasons and motivations for the breakup are operating on an unconscious level (fear). We may think that we clearly understand the reason that the union needs to be dissolved, but we really do not. We are upset, but not for the reasons we think.

In a conscious divorce, the lessons are being learned and, often, completed. We may continue in our life with no need to create similar painful relationships. However, in an unconscious divorce, this may not be the case. Since we have not clearly understood our problem, we have not yet found the solution. Until the true problem is understood and solved, we will recreate similar situations and relationships. This is not a punishment, but rather a blessing as we are given unlimited opportunities for growth.

Many people may read this book trying to determine whether they should leave a marriage or not. There is no set formula that we can use to decide. In addition to our emotions, many other factors, such as children and finances, come into play here. We can only ask for guidance to reveal to us any barriers we may have to our loving and more deeply joining with another. As we continue to seek out our own barriers to love, and release them, it may become clear to us whether we should stay or leave.

To clearly "hear" this guidance, we also must remember not to let our fears be the main decision makers, but rather our clarity and love. If we are contemplating separation, we can be overwhelmed by feelings of guilt, blame, anger, and a sense of failure. These feelings can cripple our ability to see the situation clearly and interfere with our highest inner guidance. In a highly emotional state, it is difficult to accurately assess the relationship and to determine if we should continue as mates or not. Also if our mate is still pushing our buttons in a major way, it may indicate that we have not completed our lessons with them. Once we have, we may find that we are no longer getting upset to the extent we were before. In this more peaceful state, it will be easier to understand our inner guidance.

It will be helpful if we have understood what it is within ourselves that caused us to create our pain in the relationship. This will help us avoid similar pain in the future, as well as free us from mistakenly blaming the other for our pain. If possible, it is best to continue to work with these feelings until we are blaming neither ourselves nor our mate. We need to try to answer the question "Why did I call this relationship and this person into my life?" If possible, we need to keep working on our inner process until a sense of calm pervades our decision making (the conscious divorce).

Tremendous confusion will be a part of this process and, unfortunately, the world has not given much validity to this normal human condition. Confusion is often a necessary part of decision making. Often when we bring an issue into consciousness (do I want to remain in this relationship?), we may have to pass through confusion to arrive at clarity. Most of us, and society at large, are very uncomfortable being in a state of confusion. This is often the reason that we do not bring up an issue.

The world tells us we are "adults" and we should not be confused. We should always clearly know what we want and feel. Confusion is, however, a normal, healthy state. If we accept it and keep working with it, out of this confusion will eventually emerge a course of action that appears to offer us the greatest peace. This is our Divine inner guidance.

From a state of greater clarity we will be more able to discern our true guidance. In the angry and tumultuous state under which many divorces occur, this is often very difficult to do. We must be willing to give up our attachments to the direction and outcome of this guidance. We can "listen" to our hearts as to whether we feel guided to change the relationship in its present mated form and continue it in another form. If we stop blaming ourselves and our mate and just ask, we will be answered. We need to ask, "Can I be at peace in this relationship?" Resolving our fears regarding divorce can help us reach this state of equilibrium.

We need to ask, "Can I be at peace in this relationship?"

However, we may not be able to reach this state of inner serenity before deciding. We may find it too upsetting to continue in the existing relationship. We may feel that we must physically separate to find peace. Or we may find that it is only through the process of the separation that clarity is achieved. Only after we have physically left the relationship and reflect on it do we begin to understand the forces that undermined it. If this is the case, this too must be honored. Often after separation, it may become clear that we were blaming the other for our pain and we still feel we want to separate. We can then begin to reopen our hearts to the other, but still continue on our path towards separation or divorce.

If we feel that certain important elements are missing in our marriage, we may want to ask our mate if they are willing to work on instilling these elements within the union. Perhaps we feel we need more time, more communication, more spirituality, more affection or sex, more acknowledgment, less criticism, more adventure. Whatever we feel is essential for us, we can request this from our mate and ask them to honestly answer whether they are willing to work toward providing it, whether they think it is essential or not. After hearing their honest answer, we may then more clearly be able to understand whether we can continue in a union devoid of this element. At least now we are making the decision based on an honest evaluation instead of frustrated hopes.

Common Fears Regarding Separation and Divorce

To gain greater clarity, we need to resolve our fears, at least to the point where they are not dominant in our decision. This does not mean that certain fears and upsetting emotions are not still affecting us as we try to decide. It only means that they are no longer the primary factors and do not dictate our decision and action. If they still do, then our decision to stay or leave will be based on these fears and, therefore, still be an unconscious one. Only by understanding these fears so they no longer hold such a powerful sway can we begin to free ourselves from them.

FEAR THAT SEPARATION WILL HAVE A DETRIMENTAL EFFECT ON CHILDREN: I have put this fear first as consideration for the children involved needs to be primary in our minds. We make many selfless sacrifices for our children and staying in a marriage we might otherwise leave may be one of them. Indeed, this must be taken into account as children are tremendously affected when their parents divorce. However, it should not fearfully be taken into account. Children are also tremendously affected when they are raised in a severely dysfunctional, but intact, family unit. If children are involved, well-managed coparenting can be more beneficial than staying in a home where the marriage has become constantly vindictive and hostile.

Recent research is showing that the effects of divorce has a greater impact on children than we may have previously thought. They do not "bounce back" as quickly or as completely as we had hoped. However, a divorce with dignity and calm can minimize the impact on children.

Even if only one partner can remain balanced and loving during and after a divorce, this can serve as a model to the children as to how to respond to attack and pain. It can also create at least one home environment where love, rather than fear, dominates.

However, if children are involved, especially young children, their needs, as well as those of the parents, must be taken into account. Though we are free to choose to make a mate an ex-mate, children are not free to choose to make a full-time parent into a part-time parent, who they see on weekends and holidays. The decision is made for them. And, except in cases of severe emotional or physical abuse, children will not choose to be separated from either parent. Therefore, since they are part of the family, their desires too must be considered.

Concern for their needs can lead us in either direction, towards leaving or staying. If a toxic or abusive parent is involved, it may be best that children be removed from continued exposure to them. Other times we may decide to stay when, if children were not involved, we might leave. Often we may decide to stay with someone, at least until the children are older, who is performing adequately as a parent, though perhaps not so well as a mate. Children do best in homes with a healthy balance of both male and female energy. Divorce often upsets this much-needed balance. A recent survey found that just having a father in the home, even if he was inattentive and uninvolved, had a very positive effect on children.

Separation decisions involving children at home are perhaps the most difficult and confusing ones. Children often learn major lessons by watching a parent begin to honor themselves and no longer allow a predominantly fear-based relationship to continue. Leaving or changing a toxic marriage can remind them that unhealthy life situations are under our control and can be corrected. On the other hand, watching their parents separate in an unconscious divorce often leads to greater pain and confusion. However, there may be important lessons for them here as well.

FEAR WE ARE RESPONSIBLE FOR ANOTHER'S PAIN: One major fear is that we are responsible for whatever pain another may experience should we decide to separate. A woman at a marriage seminar I led expressed this fear. She had been married over twenty years to a man she had clearly wanted to leave for many years. No children were involved, so the decision only impacted her and her husband. Her husband had had many painful events in his life which he chose to interpret as "attacks and rejections." He had come to see the world through the eyes of a victim and greatly feared any further rejections. Actually, it was his tremendous fear of rejection that had drained his wife over the twenty years of their marriage. His fear of rejection was creating just what he feared.

At this point in his life, his wife was the only close relationship he had, although "close" is not really an accurate description. She feared the pain he would experience should she also reject him. She feared it might be the final blow, perhaps "causing" him to close his heart forever. She felt guilty and responsible for his pending pain. She had become his mother, trying to keep "her child" from feeling pain. However, her desire not to see someone she loved in greater pain was only part of her hesitation. Her guilt and fear of confronting his pain and anger were the greater parts.

During the seminar she realized her leaving would not be the cause of his pain nor was she responsible for it, not matter how strongly he may feel she was. She realized that she could even respect his decision to close his heart, if he felt he could take no more chances in this lifetime.

She realized something that we all often forget and resist accepting. She realized that his pain may be necessary to motivate him to change. Usually major changes in our hearts and minds are made through our challenges and pain. If integrated internally with love and acceptance, these changes usually lead us to greater peace. Though often painful, they are not a "bad" thing, to be avoided at all costs.

We cannot take away another's pain nor should we. We never know what will bring another peace. Sometimes what will bring someone peace is the inner search motivated by a painful divorce. We do not serve another, nor their growth, by avoiding situations which they have decided will bring them pain. When we do this, we are not helping them to confront and release their fears, but rather to temporarily placate them. We become "enablers" to their addiction to fear, just as an alcoholic's spouse can become an enabler to their addiction to alcohol. We may rationalize that our guilt and fear of confronting them are expressions of love and support. We then teach fear, not love.

FEAR WE WILL BE PUNISHED FOR SEPARATING AND ARE NEVER TO KNOW MARITAL HAPPINESS: Another fear that comes to bear is that we will be punished for "deserting" the relationship, for not constantly loving them unconditionally. We feel guilty that we cannot love them purely enough to not be upset by their fearful and unloving behavior. We may fear that, should we separate, we will be deprived of any future loving mates or marital happiness for having left this relationship "unnecessarily and selfishly." Or we may fear that we may one day regret leaving, having decided we judged the other too harshly and should have stayed in the relationship.

To release these fears we need to remember that we will always create our relationships from our present belief system, not from ramifications or punishment for our past actions. God will never punish us, only heal us. Present and future happiness will not be withheld from us because of our past relationships, unless we withhold it from ourselves. If we later realize that we may have been able to stay in a relationship that we decided to leave, no regrets are necessary. There are certain lessons we needed to learn that we could only learn by leaving. Maybe one of the lessons was that we did not need to leave. However, the only way we could have learned that was by leaving. If we have truly learned these lessons, they will no longer affect our future relationships.

FEAR THAT WE DO NOT DESERVE A LOVING RELATIONSHIP: We may fear that we are not really worthy enough to ask for love and support in a relationship. We may feel that the existing union, no matter how unloving, unresponsive, or abusive, is all we deserve or is reasonable to expect in a marriage. We may mistakenly believe that no one will ever love us more, because we do not really deserve any more love. We may believe we have only two choices, a painful relationship or desolate loneliness.

There is a third choice: to begin to alter our belief system to one of believing that we deserve love and commitment. This new belief system will then create a loving relationship, either with our existing mate or a new partner. To release this fear we need only remember that God's will for us is only happiness and love. He has created us to love and be loved. All our pain lies in our forgetting this single fact.

A SMORGASBORD OF OTHER FEARS: A host of other fears can emerge as we contemplate divorce. Often these fears present themselves in a myriad of forms that often mask their true source. We may fear that if we separate, our mate may find greater happiness than we will, especially with another person. This concern is really an outgrowth of the fear that we are unlovable or may be punished for "deserting" the relationship. We may fear that if we separate, we will never get revenge. In this case we are remaining stuck in a special hate relationship.

A friend of ours was recently telling us that she felt strangely reluctant to finalize her divorce after the one-year mandatory separation expired. Her husband had initiated the separation by leaving her for another relationship. Her hesitation confused her, especially since she was in a very happy new relationship and had no desire to be with her husband again. She admitted her new relationship was much more loving and mature than her previous marriage of thirty-one years.

When I asked her why she was reluctant to finalize her divorce, she said she really did not know. I then reminded her that she really did know, but had not yet been able to consciously articulate it. So I asked her again to look deep inside and describe the feelings she was having that expressed themselves as reluctant. After a moment, she said, "I feel that if I finally divorce him, I will give up all chances of ever hearing him say he really does love me and wishes he had never left. Another feeling is that in some way the divorce seems to be a symbol of death of our family unit" (they had three grown children).

As she discussed these feelings, she realized that in many ways she had spent thirty-one years in marriage waiting to really know that he truly loved her. It now seemed fruitless to wait any longer. She released her attachment (special relationship) without hearing him say this. As with all special relationships, even had she gotten what she thought she wanted, she would have only found herself once again disappointed. She was also able to acknowledge that she did have a successful family and that it would continue. Her feelings toward her children, and their feelings toward her, had not weakened. In fact, they were much closer. The family had changed, but not disappeared. Two of the family members, the parents, were changing the form of their relationship.

The Unconscious Divorce

Above are some of the common fears that come to bear when we are considering divorcing. If fears are not resolved, they will rule our decision-making process. If this happens, the pain or exhaustion of our special love/hate relationship may become so intense or the desire to seek another romantic relationship so great that one or both of the partners may decide to "end" the relationship, rather than "complete" it. By end I do not mean divorce or separation. Divorce or separation may continue the relationship but in another form. By "end" I mean that we stop trying to restore peace and love in the relationship, in any form. We choose to close our hearts to the other person. We may do this by leaving the relationship through separation or divorce or by remaining physically but being emotionally absent (a "silent divorce").

Actually we cannot end nor complete a relationship if we still have attack thoughts toward the other. It goes with us everywhere. In truth, we never need to end the relationship, even should we decide to change its form by divorcing or separating. We may change the form of the relationship (married, separated, divorced, etc.) but its content (to teach and learn love) will always remain the same. A spouse may now be our ex-mate, but our goal to see them through the eyes of love continues.

However, we can complete a relationship by beginning to love another unconditionally, by seeing their true inner perfection. This does not mean liking them, loving them as a mate, or staying physically with them. We may still find that we need to remove ourselves physically from the relationship, either temporarily or permanently. This is only a change of form. However, even as an ex-mate, we can still strive to see their light through their painful calls for help. At times, this may be a totally internal process on our part, with little or no further actual contact with the other person.

———— ❦ ————

*A spouse may now be our ex-mate, but our goal to see them
through the eyes of love continues.*

———— ❦ ————

Trying to decide whether we should divorce or separate is one of the most difficult decisions many of us may ever have to make. Many people will never leave a marriage but they may spend a lifetime trying to decide if they should. By doing this they never commit to the relationship or its goals. On the other hand, many people would rather separate than change. For them, a change of partners may be only that.

Though there seem to be many reasons why people separate, let us look at a few common sources for unconscious divorces. In each of these cases, we may have not yet penetrated the illusion and seen the truth. The reasons we have told ourselves we are divorcing (the illusions) are in reality quite different from the real reasons (the truth).

THE PASSION IS GONE: The diminishing or ceasing of sexual passion and attraction is a common cause of divorce. If we are basing the relationship on romantic, sexual attraction, when it is gone, the relationship seems to have no basis. We decide that if this relationship can offer us no greater sexual passion and pleasuring, then we must leave it. We will look for yet another special love relationship that will rekindle our desires. Should we decide to remain in the relationship, we may feel that it is incomplete and unfulfilling, that an essential ingredient is missing.

The reason this is an unconscious motivation has been discussed in the earlier chapter on romantic love. We think we are seeking the perfect special romantic relationship, but in reality we are seeking God's love. We think that life's greatest joy will be experienced through our bodies, through sexual joining. No body or person can ever give us this feeling of oneness we are seeking. However, we may keep going from relationship to relationship, leaving when the passion dies or diminishes.

Separation based on the diminishing of sexual passion does not allow for its normal ebbing that occurs over the life of the relationship. Also, it may not allow the relationship to endure long enough for us to experienced the renewed sexual enjoyment available to us in a Stage 3 healed relationship. We have decided that a mated union is incomplete without this passion. In doing this, we have forgotten the true function of the union and replaced it with physical pleasuring and false intimacy.

BLAMING OUR MATE FOR OUR PAIN: Another reason people decide to separate is that they have judged their mate and decided that they are incapable of a peaceful, loving relationship. They are in pain and have mistakenly concluded that it is their mate's fault. The reality and the illusion of this judging of another has been discussed throughout the book. Indeed, our mate may still be unwilling to choose the peace of greater joining and it may be best to leave. However, we will be unable to perceive this if we are still condemning them and blaming them for our pain.

If we are still feeling resentment, anger, condemnation, and blame, we have once again not pierced the illusion and seen the truth. In the illusion we not only believe the other is the cause of our unhappiness (the special hate relationship) but we also expect the other to be more perfect, rather than "perfectly imperfect." In the illusion, we have misunderstood their attacks and fearful behavior, forgetting they were calls for healing and help. Until the anger and blame are resolved within us, we will be unable to understand what is true and what are our projections onto another. If unresolved, these feelings can create only an unconscious divorce.

STRESS-INDUCED SEPARATION: Stress is more and more becoming the primary factor in destroying many relationships. Often both people are working and once children are added to the family, it becomes more and more difficult to remain balanced and centered. Add to this the almost frantic pace of modern urban life and the spiritual and moral bankruptcy of our culture, and the negative forces affecting the family can become extreme.

Within this fatiguing and overwhelming environment, often the problem begins to act out within the marriage. This is not to say that there may not also be problems within the marriage itself. There usually are. But in the depleted state it becomes impossible to find the time and energy to do the work to successfully heal the relationship. We may begin to express our anger and stress at the "safest" target and that can often be our mate. This may undermine the relationship and eventually lead to separation. The irony is that this often increases, rather than decreases, the stress.

Maintaining a well-balanced, peaceful home within this culture is difficult, but never impossible. However, we must make a commitment to achieving this and making peace important. This means making both major and minor everyday decisions that reflect the answer to the question, "What will bring peace here?" This often means turning off the television, socializing less, owning less, being home more, accomplishing less, not overpopulating and overscheduling our lives, etc. These are often the things that we do not want to do because we have not made peace important.

THE PERIOD OF DISCOMFORT: As mentioned earlier, many people separate during the period of discomfort. Both may have decided to commit to the goal of the healed relationship, but they did not understand the dynamics that come to bear during the period of discomfort and the crisis of faith. During these periods, the relationship will become distressed and disjointed. The intensity of the arguing may become greater than ever. This is because the structure of the relationship is not aligned with the new goal. Though stressful, these changes are positive. As with many physical healings, it may get worse before it gets better. Many leave the relationship during this period, though this is never needed!

The Conscious Divorce

As mentioned earlier, the creation of a healed relationship requires three conditions. These include: (1) a commitment to the relationship, (2) commitment to a deeper stage of joining, and (3) beginning to see our partner's interests as our own (the Golden Rule). The healed or conscious divorce has two similar conditions: (1) we strive (and hopefully succeed!) to see the other through the eyes of love, and (2) the true reasons for leaving are clear to us. To a certain degree, the three conditions of the healed marriage remain in a healed divorce, only expressed in a different form.

Conscious divorce often results when one partner is unwilling to commit to the three conditions and goals of the healed marriage. Remember, all of these conditions are essential for both to experience the healed union. Again, at a deeper level the relationship is "healed" when only one person deliberately chooses these goals. That person has brought the relationship from illusion to truth, from special to healed. However, only one is choosing to accept the peace of this healed relationship.

Often this state will create the environment for the other to make the same commitment. However, each person must decide if their partner's commitment is necessary for them to continue as mates and, if it is, how long they are willing to wait for the other to choose peace.

Losing sight of the commitment and goal will surely happen temporarily for each person as faith is built. That is to be expected and should not cause us to abandon the relationship, though we may often feel tempted to. However, we may sense that the deep bond between us and our mate to work things out is gone and in its place is a sense of separateness, perhaps even hostility. This may be happening on an unconscious level and may be unspoken. We may only be able to determine if this bond is gone by relying on our intuition and inner guidance. If we are in a state of emotional turmoil, this clear guidance will be difficult to perceive.

To seek greater joining and peace a person must commit also to their own growth. This is the only way they can discover the barriers they have erected to joining. Often one partner is on a more accelerated emotional and/or spiritual growth path than the other. If this is the case, then perhaps their growth and example can kindle this commitment in the other. Perhaps or perhaps not; it is always the other's choice, not ours.

As we remove our barriers and love unconditionally, we will heal, as will our relationship with our mate. This may or may not create the environment in which our mate can begin to heal and commit to the mutual goals. They may still need to remain in a fear-based relationship. A love-based relationship may offer too great a threat to their ego's belief system.

For the partner who is growing and releasing their fears, the fear-based patterns of behavior that have been set in place over the course of the special relationship are no longer tolerable. These fear-based patterns can range from extreme abuse to mild codependency. As one person realizes they are no longer willing to participate in the old fearful behavior, the other, who is still comfortable with it, may become distressed and/or angry. They become angry because if you no longer share their thought system, you weaken it. Those who still believe in it perceive this as an attack on them.

We may sense that our mate's need to stay in a fear-based relationship is so deep-rooted that we feel we are no longer willing to remain physically in the relationship, waiting for them to choose otherwise. Without guilt, resentment, or anger we can decide to separate. We have freed ourselves from our fears to the point where only a predominantly love-based relationship is acceptable to us. We can compassionately understand their decision to continue in a fear-based relationship. After all, until recently, we may have felt that way ourselves.

Chapter 12

Creating Miracles

*O*ur true value as miracle-workers became clear to me when a friend came to me for counseling. She was trying to determine why she had not, at the age of forty-four, created the loving mated relationship she had always longed for. All other areas of her life were bringing her peace and joy. She loved her work as a college professor. She was healthy and had a full life of loving friends and relatives. Yet she felt that there was something profoundly missing from her life and that she could not know true happiness until she had found the mate and relationship she sought. She had begun to feel, and fear, that her present life was just a series of incomplete days waiting until her "real life" could begin with her mate.

Trying to be a good counselor, I tried to help her recognize any fears that might be blocking her from creating the relationship she wanted, so she could finally be happy and at peace. Then a moment occurred in our discussion that brought tears to both of us and allowed her to release her pain and loneliness. As we talked about our true ability to create miracles in every moment, with every person, in every relationship, in every situation, twenty-four hours a day, seven days a week, 365 days a year, we both, simultaneously, had a profound realization. We realized how incredibly beautiful each moment of each day can be if we offer the miracles our love can bring. We also realized that this beauty is not dependent on, or diminished by, our marital status or any other outward condition. We are so much grander than whatever emotions we are experiencing about our love life. Every day she had the God-given ability to create miracles. We both understood that she no longer needed to wait to meet the "right man" for her "real life" and happiness to begin. It could start right now and for her it did. Perhaps it is not coincidence that when I saw her a year later, she was both happy and happily married.

Everyone would like to create miracles in their lives. It is easy to think of such wonderful things we could create and the pain we could relieve if only we were able to create miracles. We could resolve all conflicts in peace and harmony, heal sickness, create abundance, and transform all relationships into ones of love. As we begin to understand who we are and what a miracle is, we will understand that we can create them. It is as natural as breathing. In fact it is so natural that when we are not creating miracles, something has gone wrong.

However, before proceeding, a new definition of miracles is required, along with an understanding of some of the principles under which they operate. The most commonly accepted definition of miracles, that of supernatural acts of external phenomena, is not what is intended here. If miracles are interpreted as supernatural or unnatural acts, we will always doubt their reality. If they are credited to the world of divine beings, creating them will seem unattainable. They will engender fear, if they are perceived as the creation of some sinister or random force. They will be easily dismissed, if they are perceived as feats of magic or illusion. Any of these responses is understandable given our existing definition and interpretation of miracles.

However, a reinterpretation is offered. A miracle is anything and everything that comes from love, unconditional love. Miracles are all expressions of love and all expressions of love are miracles. They are simply the acts of love that we might never otherwise term as miracles, though occasionally their results may appear so incredible as to be considered "miraculous." Miracles seem rare or nonexistent only because we have misunderstood what they are and have considered them "supernatural." In truth they are very natural. When they are not occurring, we have left our "natural state" of offering unconditional love.

Miracles do not defy the laws of nature but they do defy the belief systems we have formed about the world and therefore appear "not to be part of any known natural law." We have come to believe giving means to sacrifice and lose something. The world tells us that what we have is diminished if we give. Miracles remind us that giving means getting and expanding. Miracles, acts of love, bring more love to both the receiver and the giver and in doing so reverse the "laws" of the world. In truth, it is only through this giving that love can expand. Any idea that is shared is not diminished, but rather increased. "Giving" here is not loss but gain. We can only have more by giving more. That is why in the "real" world of love, giving and receiving are the same. That is why life is "for giving."

We have come to believe we can only exert a limited control over our lives by the use of our will, desires, and personal power. Miracles remind us that we can create our lives totally through our love. We can positively influence the outcome of all situations if we offer the miracle of love in each of them. Healing will have occurred, even if the outcome does not fit the form we pictured or anticipated. Miracles remind us that we are not just bodies and egos, but limitless miracle-workers.

Miracles are a transition of illusion (fear) into truth (love). They occur when we change our minds about others, ourselves, and the world, so that we perceive them, not through our ego's eyes of fearful perceptions, but through the loving eyes of God (unconditional love). This new perception undoes the error of our perceiving ourselves as separate and allows us to see the reality of our joining and union. Miracles are accomplished by the Creator through us and in doing so, they bring healing. God loves the world through us.

Everyday Miracles

Everyone has the ability to create miracles. However, we must first alter our emotions and our belief systems so that our unconditional love can be expressed, if only briefly. However, it is not necessary for all parties involved in a relationship to be willing to offer unconditional love. Only one person must be "miracle-minded" for the miracle to occur and have its healing effects. Only the sender(s) needs to be miracle-minded, and then only briefly. In fact, the purpose of the miracles is to restore both the receiver and the sender to their right mind (miracle-mindedness). The sender temporarily has greater clarity than the receiver. Since at a very real level all minds are joined, the love unites all parties. The miracle places your mind in a state of grace and welcomes the "stranger" you earlier perceived outside of you within you as your friend.

Every day, every hour, we are able to create miracles in our lives. We are miracle-workers, cocreators of our world, and yet our egos have convinced us we are something much less than this. Many of these miracles appear as minor everyday events. A young child bumps us and we respond with a loving pat on the head instead of the expected rebuff. We take a moment to listen to the concerns of a friend or stranger and respond in a supportive, nonjudgmental manner. We signal for someone to pull ahead of us in traffic with a smile. We encourage love and forgiveness to express itself in a relationship previously dominated by resentment and conflict. We hug our children and show concern for our mate. We forgive a long-held hurt and feel free to love that person again. All these acts of love are miracles that teach love. We have chosen, perhaps unconsciously, to perceive persons and situations through God's eyes.

I recently had an opportunity to offer a miracle in an everyday situation. One rainy day I was looking for a parking space near a restaurant. I was late for my meeting and under the influence of two cups of coffee. I made a maneuver in the parking lot that, though not dangerous, was inconsiderate and scared a man driving with his family. He thought I was going to cut in front of him, but I did not. Even so, he was upset. As we walked across the parking lot he yelled at me, which I ignored and sulked off.

We both entered the same restaurant and our tension followed us in. I could barely pay attention to my lunch meeting. We were both feeling justified in our anger toward each other. After all, he thought I might have endangered his family. I felt he had yelled at me for fear of my doing something I never actually did. As my anger and upset subsided, I realized this was an opportunity to teach love and joining, not fear and separation.

I walked over to his table. His back was to me but his wife saw me approach and touched his arm, as if to warn him. He turned toward me and peered at me with angry eyes. His entire family was glaring at me. I said, "I am sorry that I was inconsiderate in the parking lot and did something that might have created a danger. I let my hurry and two cups of coffee get the better of me." Immediately everyone relaxed. He said he understood and his teenage son was driving and with the rain, he too was more nervous than usual. He apologized for yelling and everyone laughed.

Later as he left the restaurant, he stopped at my table. He said, "I want to thank you for coming over to apologize. My children learned something as important as good driving skills today." We smiled at each other and shook hands. I felt as though we had been friends for life. A miracle had replaced separation with joining and made friends of enemies.

At first, these mundane situations may appear too ordinary to be classified as miracles, but remember that a miracle is any act of unconditional love. Often small kindnesses can have a long-lasting, almost miraculous effect on our lives. We can all remember when a stranger or friend paid us a compliment or did us a kind deed. We can remember the sense of support and love we felt from key people in our lives who loved us unconditionally, causing us to love ourselves and others more. And as we loved others more, they in turn loved others more. And on and on, like a ripple in a lake when a stone has been cast, only this ripple does not end at the shore. It goes on forever. We never know who our "miracles" will affect and how. Often the results are unobservable. But all acts of love begin a cycle of healing. In this way they are all miracles and we are all potential miracle-workers.

We have endless opportunities to offer miracles in our mated relationships. There is no way to guarantee or predict what other miracles will occur from our acts of love. The other person may not outwardly change at all or may change drastically or slowly. Since the miracle has taught love, people witnessing the miracle may be moved by it and encouraged to act similarly in their relationships. In this way it may create undreamed-of changes in the lives of people we have never met.

These miracles have a great power and are different from all the other possible responses to the situation. It would be easy to dismiss miracles as just the most loving response and different only because of this. However, miracles are much more than this. Miracles allow the Creator's will to work through us in the situation. This response is different from all others in that it is the only response that we were sent to offer and the only one that can offer correction and peace. By responding from love we are responding from our true nature and allowing our Divine Will, not our ego's will, to affect the results. In doing so, we have allowed the most powerful force in nature, Love, to manifest itself. No matter how it may initially appear, it will offer us peace. All other responses will offer us conflict and illusion.

I recently received a letter from a reader of my first book, *In the Spirit of Business,* which applies these principles to our work lives. Her story is a good example of a miracle. She wrote:

"I have to tell you that just after reading this book, I was treated with enormous rudeness by a coworker. Rather than cause a scene, I quickly walked away from the conversation. She called after me in schoolteacher fashion, '*Don't* you walk away from me when I am talking to you.' Then she told my department head that I had an 'attitude problem.' *Wow!* Talk about furious! I seethed for hours, dreamed up sharp retorts for this woman all evening, and finally calmed down enough to reach for your book.

"Finally it seeped into my brain. This woman is always abrasive and overbearing, but that isn't something my words can fix. She hasn't reached any better level of relating to people. As the book noted, you don't get angry at a one-year-old for not being able to tie shoelaces; that's a skill they haven't developed, so you overlook it and tie it for them.

"Since the words wouldn't help, I decided I had to do something visual to clear the air. With a pounding heart, and hardly believing I was doing this insane thing (was I really transformed enough to react well if she started yelling again?), I took the woman flowers the next day and suggested we had gotten off to a bad start and should wipe the slate clean. She was obviously astonished, and has treated me civilly ever since. I was/am impressed by the total lack of leftover anger in me (and her) the instant we found the peace of deciding to let go of the incident and let it be done for both of us."

For a brief moment, this woman offered unconditional love and accepted the other as she was. By offering this act of love a miracle occurred in their relationship. The miracle corrected the perception of both so that they might see each other through the eyes of love. The miracle transformed their special hate relationship into an expression of healing and forgiveness.

We do not need to determine if we are ready to perform miracles. They should be involuntary, arising from our natural acts of love. If we consciously try to determine the outcome of a "miracle," we will be operating from the ego and will block the miracle from occurring. To be truly miracle-minded means simply to love unconditionally and to not be attached to the outcome or that one even be observable.

If we are trying to decide whether we are "pure" enough, we must remember that it is God that performs the miracle through us. We only need to be in a "miracle-minded" (loving) state, however briefly. Nor do we need to determine the ability of another to receive the miracle. We do not need to seek out miracles to perform, but only ask to be guided to them. We do not need to plan the results of the miracles or be attached to the outcome. We only need to ask that we see the person or situation through God's eyes, through unconditional love. We need to confirm that we want only peace here and that we do not know what will bring peace but that Spirit does. This perception will allow the miracle to manifest.

There are many different responses available to us as we interact with our mates and others. Only one response, the miracle, will offer peace and healing. If this is truly the result we desire then our choice is clear. We must relinquish our faulty perceptions made by our fears and judgments and substitute for this the compassion, clarity, and gentleness offered by Love (God). Every day we can perform miracles. Every day we can know peace.

Chapter 13

Our Best Marriage Counselors

I must admit this was my hardest chapter to work on. I know this is because I still have such resistance to solving my dilemmas with anything other than my intellect, my will, and my ego. However, at a deep level I know that this will not produce the clear and loving resolutions that can be brought forward by asking to have God's will work through us, not our own. I know this and yet I resist it. My ego is hard pressed to give up any of its well-entrenched turf. So I confess this chapter reflects the hypocrisy of a well-intentioned truth.

Most of us seek out various "counselors" to help us solve the problems created during the power struggle of Stage 2. The sources include friends, professional counselors, books, our mates, seminars, and our own inner processing. Depending on their clarity, these sources can be helpful or hurtful to us in creating a peaceful relationship. It is not unusual for us to seek out a source that will agree with our conclusions, which is often that the problems are our mate's fault. We all like agreement for the justification for our anger and attack. At times we all feel we are the victim. There are, however, two excellent "counselors" available to us twenty-four hours a day, 365 days a year, free of charge: God and our Higher Self.

In the Western world, where the ego is held in such high esteem, the idea of allowing anything other than the ego to control our lives and thoughts is seen as a weakness. The concept of turning our relationships over to anyone and anything other than ourselves seems dangerous and personally insulting to most of us. But in reality we have already turned our lives over to something other than our true self. We have turned our lives over to our egos, which have made a mess of them. Turning our lives over to God and our Higher Self is not turning it over to someone or something outside ourselves, but rather it is returning the control to our true self. We are reinstating our internal authority of this self, while removing it from the fearful illusions of our egos, our false self.

The ego will continue to tell us that we do not really need Divine assistance to form a totally loving and peaceful relationship. Indeed, the ego's function is to deny the need for this. We will tell ourselves that if we just were to meet the right person, who totally loved us and was free of most emotional problems, then we could have the perfect relationship. Or perhaps we will tell ourselves if we just developed better communication techniques, or greater sexual compatibility or got to more counseling or more workshops, or resolve more of our inner conflict, we will eventually transform ourselves and our existing special relationships into ones of true fulfillment and lasting peace. Or maybe we think if we meditate long enough and exercise hard enough and eat the right foods and think the right thoughts, we will purify ourselves enough to deserve and be able to create the perfect relationship.

Though all of these things can be of value, none of them individually, nor all of them together, will ever be able to create the healed relationship. Without God's guidance and help we cannot do it. This is because the essential nature and elements of a healed relationship is an awareness and a manifestation of the functions assigned it by God, even if this is happening at an unconscious level. This is accomplished by welcoming God into our marriage and asking that it be used for His purposes, rather than those of the ego. When we love unconditionally, when we practice the Golden Rule, we are welcoming God in, even if we do not yet believe in Him. We are teaching love, not fear; joining, not separation. By doing so, we have become teachers of God.

———— ✤ ————

God will transform our special relationships into healed relationships.

———— ✤ ————

God will not destroy or end our special relationships. Rather, He will transform them into healed and holy ones. God will purify them and remove as much fear as we allow Him. He will use our special relationships, no matter how confused and painful they may have become, as teaching aids and learning experiences to demonstrate the truth of unconditional love.

We can seek God's guidance in our lives by welcoming Him in. It takes only a little willingness on our part and God will do the rest. He has told us that certainty of faith is not necessary, only a little willingness. We only need "the faith of a mustard seed." We do not have to have all hatred, fear, and guilt removed from our minds. That is God's function. We are not asked to have a constant or even strong belief that God exists and can help. God understands that we are completely worthy of all the good that He wills for us. We will be guided through the plan that He wants us to follow in every situation and relationship. If we are willing to turn our special relationships over to Him, God will use them as teaching aids to teach love.

Asking God to heal our relationships and marriage is not a difficult process of memorizing rituals or years of purification and devotion. After asking, we can go right back to judging and fighting. But once God has been asked in, He cannot be ushered back out. It is simply the asking of His assistance and then being willing, if only briefly, to have Him change our perceptions. God is not looking at your mate and thinking, "How uncommunicative they are." Or "What a neurotic, emotionally insecure person they are." God sees only our real self, guiltless and flawless. We can see our mates (and everyone else) through His perception if we will only ask. We can ask Him to heal our relationships, realizing that we do not know how. The struggle is not in asking Him, but rather in arriving at the point of clarity and acceptance to know Who to ask and why.

The true source of our inner wisdom is our Higher Self or our true self, which is our true identity as a Child of God. In various teachings this has been referred to as the Higher Power, Universal Consciousness, Holy Spirit, Inner Divinity, Cosmic Consciousness, God Consciousness, and a host of other terms that all refer to the same essence of our nature. This self is contrasted to our "ego self," which we made as a substitute for this Higher Self. As we release our fears, this Higher Self, which is the love God has instilled in us, emerges from behind the clouds of fear. We can then ask this Higher Self to manifest in our lives and relationships.

Asking for Guidance: How Do We Do It?

Asking for Divine direction and guidance may be a rather easy concept to understand, but how do we actually do this? The answer to this is also easy to understand, but more difficult to implement. However, in reality not to allow this guidance to direct us is much more difficult. This is shown by the present painful condition of our lives, which have been guided by our egos, our false self. Manifesting our Higher Self is the goal on the planet, a demanding but miraculous and joyous endeavor. It is a process of remembering and self-discovery. Its immediate reward is greater personal peace and clarity. Its ultimate gift is complete freedom and union, which is the "Atonement." It is a lifetime challenge.

Determining this guidance is arrived at in several ways. It differs for everyone, as different teaching aids will work for different people. However, there are some common processes that are commonly used.

RELEASING OUR FEARS: On an everyday level, this Divine guidance will manifest more and more as we resolve and release our fears. Any peaceful, loving thought is coming from our Higher Self. As our fears are reduced, our Love, which is our Higher Self, will illuminate our thoughts and feelings. These will be transformed from predominantly fear-based to predominantly love-based. As we remove our fears and barriers to joining, the guidance will flow into our minds. Then our actions, which are predicated on these thoughts and feelings, will reflect greater clarity and love. These actions, based on love, are miracles. These miracles, these everyday acts of love, are manifesting our Higher Self.

It is often the case that guidance is made clear with a multi-step process. After a period of striving and honest self-exploration to understand and release our fears regarding the situation, these fears will have receded to a degree where they no longer dominate our thinking. At this stage of our spiritual development it becomes easier and easier to quiet our minds, as the shouting of our fears has abated.

This is not to say that all fear must be resolved before we can find a loving mate or transform our existing relationship into a peaceful one. Only a cruel God could create a world where all fear must be resolved for us to be free of pain or have our most deeply felt desires answered. God is not cruel and loves us totally and unconditionally. A loving Creator would not create us with an intense desire for a loving mated relationship without also providing each of us the means for this desire to be satisfied.

MEDITATION OR REFLECTION: Usually beginning and ending the day with periods of quiet reflection and/or meditation are helpful in stilling the incessant rambling of our ego minds, so that this guidance can be "sensed." This process can include a disciplined meditation technique or simply sitting quietly and praying or thinking loving thoughts. We may want to reflect on the past to determine what we have learned and where we could have loved more. We may turn towards the future and begin to visualize peaceful, happy outcomes in the situations ahead. This process is also helpful for reducing stress and quieting fears.

INTUITION: Some people perceive this guidance by hearing a voice or seeing a visual image in their mind. But this is rather rare. Often our intuitive hunches or our "sense" of something are being guided by our Higher Self. We just have "a feeling" that we should do a certain thing or that a certain thing is about to occur. Often, we might feel guided to follow a certain path for no "rational" reason. It just feels right. However, these intuitive suggestions can often be affected by our insecurities or desires. Therefore, we must strive to put these at peace within ourselves as much as possible.

SEEKING PEACE AND HEALING: Also, we will be seeking the most loving and healing course of action in any given situation. We will be seeking a course that has as its goal only love and healing of all involved. We must ask ourselves if this action will instill peace in ourselves and others, even if it initially threatens our egos. Any course of action based on our desire to join and heal will cause no injury even though others may decide to react to it fearfully.

As we seek such a course, many others will be eliminated, especially those based on our fears and having guilt and attack as their goal. From the few remaining, one will usually be made clear to us by our experience of a sense of serenity, and perhaps joy and anticipation, as we contemplate following it. It will be the path "with heart." The process demands clarity of emotion and purpose. This is the difficult part and the decision will reflect this clarity (or lack of it).

Resistance may surface at the idea that all we want from a relationship or situation is God's peace. There are many other things we may "think" we want. Our goals may include "love," pleasure, conquest, money, attention, superiority, satisfaction, security, punishment, recognition, adulation, and a host of other things we think we "need." However, reason will tell us that we only want these things because we hope they will bring us a sense of peace and wholeness. To make peace our priority does not mean that we must abandon all these other things. However, if peace is our first priority, no action or response will be acceptable to us unless peace is one of the outcomes. If you are still resisting this idea, try to remember that peace has no cost to anyone and that it can only bless. No sacrifice is involved here. Therefore, our only request needs to be for God's answer and peace.

SHARING OUR STORIES: Often Divine guidance is communicated as we honestly share our life stories and explain what we learned with each other. As we tell another our story, or as we listen to theirs, we "enter" the story and the lessons are communicated to each other. As we share these lessons, and tell and hear what has worked, we will often feel guided. I have used many stories throughout this book, both mine and those of others, as I feel our stories are one of the most powerful teaching aids.

PRAYER: Usually when we think of prayers, we think of prayers of supplication and intercession. We plead with God to give us what we want. This may be anything from a cure for our illness to a new car. This is one type of prayer. However, our most deeply felt emotions and our strongest desires are another type of prayer, though we have seldom acknowledged them as such. We are always receiving from an abundant universe, and a benevolent Creator, exactly what we are asking and praying for. We have complete freedom to create whatever we desire. The problem is we are not always clear that we are praying or what we are praying for.

The prayers that we are directing towards what we hope is a responsive and generous God are not the brief supplications and requests we make before meals and sleep. Nor are they the intense pleading that we make in times of great pain or fear. Our prayers are rather the constant stream of thoughts and feelings that pour forth from us on an ongoing basis in each and every area of our lives.

If our constant flow of emotions and thoughts in regard to our marriages is that we cannot have or do not deserve a loving relationship, our "prayer" will be answered and we will not have one. On the other hand, if we feel we do deserve one and that we can create one, this "prayer" too will be answered. A careful observation of our marriages, and marriages we observe, will show the validity of this concept. Our "prayers" are always answered as we create each area of our lives from our belief systems.

Perhaps we are alone and have been praying to find the "right mate." We think if we can only pray hard enough, and purely enough, our prayer will be answered. In truth what we only need to do is to understand and release the barriers (fears) that we have in regard to our mated relationships so that our love and trust can emerge. This prayer of love and faith will then be answered, instead of our prayer of fear. Our prayer here can be to reveal to us and to heal all the blocks that may be still within us that prevent us from finding a loving mate.

The words we use to pray may play no part in the prayer's effectiveness. It is rather the prayer of the heart that is answered. Sometimes these prayers match the words we are using; other times, they do not. Often our heart is more fearful than trusting. Often our prayerful words belie our true feelings. Words can be helpful in assisting us on focusing and concentrating on heartfelt prayers. However, it is only the true emotions that the words are imbued with that have an effect.

This also explains why the Bible says all prayers are answered and yet we perceive that many prayers go unanswered. True prayers are always answered, though the answer may not fit the outcome our egos had "prayed" for. Often the answer that the ego prays for, for example those regarding physical healing, would offer a frightening threat to us if they were answered. Should we be miraculously healed of our illness, this may offer such a great threat to our belief system about how the body works and the reality of Divine healing that our fears would be greatly increased. We may not yet be ready to believe that we can be healed. No prayer will be answered by Spirit that will increase our fears since it is the release of these fears toward which He is guiding us. We may not yet be willing to accept that we are holy Children of God and that He dwells within us and can heal us.

Once we have begun to understand how prayer works, we may not have yet understood its true purpose and proper use. At first we may use it as a tool of our egos to create what it wants. We have learned that as we let go of our fears and replace them with faith (in ourselves, the universe, God, etc.) in any area of our life, we can create what we want in that area, whether that be a mate, money, healing, success, etc. We have learned that if we change our minds we can change our lives.

Usually we misunderstand the source of this power and its ability to create and thereby use this law to serve the desires and perceived needs of our ego. We assume that we (our egos) are the source of our power and success. Indeed, this misunderstanding is an inevitable step on our path towards true understanding. For a time, this path leads to the glorification of the individual ego, arrogance, and a reinforcing of the illusion that we are all separate and have created ourselves. This is the predicament of many of the leaders in business and politics, fields that tend to attract fixed and well-defined egos. They have not yet understood the true source and the intended purpose of their power of creation and prayer.

The highest form of prayer, "true" prayer, comes from recognizing that God and Higher Self, not our petty little egos, are the source of all creation. True prayer goes a step further than acknowledging the Source of all our answers. It is also an awareness that we do not know what will bring peace in any situation. It acknowledges that we have no way of knowing the best outcome or "form" the answer will take. Our egos will pray for certain outcomes we desire (physical healing, financial success, marital bliss, etc.). However, these are all results on the physical plane to which we are attached.

Understanding this, the clearest use of prayer then is neither to plead with a capricious God nor to use our creative abilities in the service of the ego. The true use of prayer is to communicate with our Creator. Through this prayer we receive love from the Creator. Through our miracles, our acts of love and forgiveness, this love is then expressed and passed on to others. The clearest prayer, with regard to our relationship with our mates, is to seek communication with our Creator and ask that we be vehicles of this love to our mates and all others.

We must relinquish our attachment to any particular outcome and recognize that we do not know what will bring peace. A particular desired outcome represents concern for the form. Asking that God's love and peace manifest corrects this by focusing instead on content.

Trust in God's strength and ability to answer all prayer for the highest good of all involved means relinquishing of all attachments to the actual results or outcome. Our prayer is for peace to manifest in this situation and then release it as we do not know what will bring peace. In relationships, our prayer is to see the other person through God's eyes. This is the same as asking that our perception of the other be changed so that the relationship can be healed.

Indeed the only real prayer is for forgiveness. It is an asking for "forgive-ness" that is a restoring to our mind the understanding that we already have everything we need, that nothing has been taken from us. Nothing is lacking. This awareness leads us to the realization that there is nothing else but this understanding that we need to pray for.

When we are "asking out of need," it acknowledges our weakness and indicates that we have forgotten who we truly are, Divine miracle-workers. True prayer asks only that we accept what has already been given, that we receive what is already there. Why ask for anything when we have everything already? Eventually our prayers can reach a formless state and can become communication with God. Indeed we do not even need to seek a response from "outside" our minds as this only serves to continue the illusion of separation. It is only since we believe ourselves to be separate from Heaven that Heaven presents itself to us as a separate God (Jesus, Buddha, etc.). Why ask for advice for a problem of short duration when we are offered eternity, wherein all answers are contained? This is why we are told to seek first the Kingdom, all else will be given to us. When we seek the love of Heaven, we have everything.

The Practical Application of Guidance

Other than an overall asking of God to reinterpret our relationship (or to guide us to one), we can ask for assistance at any time. For example, if you find yourself angry as your mate, even if you think it is justifiable anger (and everyone thinks their anger is justifiable), you can ask God to change your perceptions of the person and the situation. Then, with an open heart, just allow yourself to see things differently. If you are sincere in your asking, it will not take long.

Often we can torture ourselves trying to determine if we are really sensing true guidance or rather just sending signals to ourselves from our egos and our desires, and then rationalizing that they are from God. We worry, "How do I really know this is Divine guidance? Am I really 'pure' enough yet to intuit it?" Some people hear an actual voice, but most of us are left with more vague promptings that we have to muddle through.

In truth we have been hearing God's voice all our lives. God is talking to us all day long. We just do not choose to listen. Hearing God's voice is usually not a mystical, transcendental experience. It is the prompting we feel to love and give and treat others kindly. It is simply our asking to understand, and then expressing unconditional love in our everyday interactions with others. The key is to ask, quietly listen as best we can at the moment, and proceed with the guidance that we feel offers us the greatest peace and solace.

We do not need to wait until we are "pure and perfect" to act on this guidance. It may or may not be heavily influenced by our egos. We may not be able to evaluate that until a later time. We can just go ahead and act, trusting that we are receiving the best guidance that we are able to understand at the time, and be willing to learn if we later find out it was influenced by our fears and desires.

Also, though it is best to make available several times in the day to sit quietly and ask for guidance, this may not always be possible. Sometimes we may need guidance immediately. When these immediate situations occur, we know that we can quickly ask for guidance and we will feel instantly prompted. True guidance is available to us in whatever time frame is available.

It is important to understand that we can ask for guidance for all our decisions, large and small. It is easier for us to accept that we can ask for guidance in our "important" decisions, who to marry, what job to accept, what healing path to pursue, how to forgive, etc. However, we can ask for guidance in every decision, no matter how small or unimportant it appears. God is not rushed and cannot be "imposed upon" by our frequent requests.

The reason to ask for guidance in small matters is twofold. First, we will be guided so as to save time. In this way we avoid getting bogged down in the minutiae and do not waste our time and energy on trivia. If for instance we are looking to purchase an item, we can ask which store to go to. By quieting ourselves, we may be able to "sense" the answer. Rather than having to search for what we need, we will be guided directly to it.

The second reason to ask for guidance on "unimportant" details is that He may direct us in such a way that we encounter someone by "accident" who truly needs our help. Perhaps in the store we enter into a conversation with the clerk, or we meet a friend or a stranger in the parking lot. God may have some message or answer to bring to them through our conversation. Perhaps we just smile at someone or treat a child kindly who bumps into us. He will provide us endless opportunities to heal ourselves and others all during the day and even in the most common and "unimportant" circumstances.

We can start our days by quietly asking God to guide us throughout. We can give each day to Him. We will be guided to certain individuals so that we can learn the lessons for the day together. Everyone will be sent to us with a learning goal of love already set, and one which can be learned that day. Each day we will be "told" what our role is to be and how we might create greater love and peace. We need only ask to see each person as God would see them and to remember that in every encounter, we are meeting another Child of God. We should not leave the meeting without blessing them and, by doing so, we are blessed.

We do not need to be pure to ask Holy Spirit for help. In fact we are told to bring our impurities (our anger, dishonesty, unkindness, etc.) to Him, as He is the purifier. We need only ask that He change our hearts and minds and express a willingness to be free of these painful feelings. God cannot help unless we ask as we are beings of free will and God can only intervene if we freely ask. And if we ask, God will offer us freedom and joy.

Chapter 14

Our Union: A Gift to the World

*I*n a marriage, where interaction is continuing over a long period of time and emotions are intense and deeply felt, our mate is truly our savior and teacher. Indeed, we have chosen them as such but temporarily forgot and believed them to serve many other functions. In truth, they have only one and that they share with every other person on our planet. We are all ministers to each other, for like all clerics, our function is to remind us of our innate spiritual nature.

The temple of our spirit is neither a building nor our bodies, but rather our relationships. It is only through relationships that we can attain our "salvation" from fear and illusion. It is only through our relationships that we find "at-one-ment" with our Creator and each other. The healed relationship, where unconditional love is encouraged and flourishes, is God's love expressed through us to others. We cannot truly and totally accept our own innocence and Divinity unless and until we see it in another person and they in turn see it in us. It is a condition of human existence that   we need this external validation to be truly convinced.

By witnessing the healing effects the miracles of our love are having on others, we are offered the proof we need as to our own spiritual perfection. Conversely, by having someone else see our holiness we are further convinced. This process becomes beautifully cyclical and spins an aura of healing around the relationship. In our marriages we can create a beautiful spiral of love and forgiveness as we each perceive the other's inner light. As we see past the veil of their appearances and see the beauty and light in our partner, they experience a healing flowing from us to them. Their own vision then becomes clearer and they are more able to see our inner perfection. As they do, we then become healed and clearer, once again better able to see their light. This experience of giving and receiving continues to quicken and deepen, and leads eventually, and inevitably, to the accomplishment of the healed relationship.

The Sacred Function

We have been called together to the most sacred function this world knows. This sacred function of marriage and of all relationships is for them to be healed and to express and extend the unconditional love of God. This is the expression of God's love on earth. It is meant to be shared, not just between the two people involved, but with everyone who is drawn into our lives. This is preparation for our experiencing God's love directly.

The function of the holy relationship is not to exclude others from our newfound peace and clarity. This would simply become another special relationship. In truth, the function of all healed relationships is to share them with the world. We begin to love our partner as a symbol for all humanity. Eventually we can learn to love everyone as the healed relationship has shown us how to love our partner. It is as if the work we do with our mates to free ourselves from our fears is shared with everyone we encounter.

It may sound absurd to say the goal is to love our car mechanic as we love our mate, but that is exactly the goal. This does not diminish the value and beauty of our love for our mate by bringing it down to the level of our feelings toward a casual acquaintance. Rather it elevates the way we love the casual acquaintance to the level of God's love that we now offer our mate. This is the true function of the healed relationship, to express unconditional love and extend this out into the world.

As we commit to a healed relationship and advance towards its accomplishment, God will be able to use our healed marriages more and more to help awaken others and offer them comfort and solace. This is always happening, both for us as individuals and for our relationships, even when they are special relationships. However, this process is greatly accelerated and intensified as we move towards a healed relationship. Not only are both partners perceiving the world and people around them with greater clarity and love but their newfound capability to offer true forgiveness can be quickly and effectively utilized to help many others.

The temple of our spirit is neither a building nor our bodies, but rather our relationships.

We do not need to go out and seek others with whom to share our love. They will be sent to us. There will be those who, because of their present level of understanding, can best accept and understand our particular form of teaching the universal truths of love. The teaching aids and language we may use speaks to them. They have accepted us as teachers, as we have them. We do not need to be attached to who they are or the form of the service we may offer to them. Often it is greatly different from what we had envisioned. At every stage we, and they, will be guided to the relationship that best serves the highest good of all involved. There are no accidents in God's plan and those who are to meet will meet, because together they have the potential for the healed relationship.

There is no one who needs to be excluded from our holy relationship as it extends. Everyone is worthy of love and everyone can teach us love.